*"God loves me. And all God
does is for my own good."*
Anthony T. Rossi

ANTHONY T. ROSSI

CHRISTIAN & ENTREPRENEUR

The Story of the Founder of
Tropicana

Sanna Barlow Rossi

INTERVARSITY PRESS
DOWNERS GROVE, ILLINOIS 60515

InterVarsity Press is the book-publishing division of InterVarsity Christian Fellowship, a student movement active on campus at hundreds of universities, colleges and schools of nursing. For information about local and regional activities, write Public Relations Dept., InterVarsity Christian Fellowship, 6400 Schroeder Rd., P.O. Box 7895, Madison, WI 53707-7895.

Distributed in Canada through InterVarsity Press, 860 Denison St., Unit 3, Markham, Ontario L3R 4H1, Canada.

ISBN 0-8308-4999-8

Printed in the United States of America

Library of Congress Cataloging in Publication Data

Rossi, Sanna Barlow.
    Anthony T. Rossi, Christian and entrepreneur.

    1. Rossi, Anthony T.   2. Baptists—United States—
Biography.   3. Businessmen—United States—Biography.
4. Tropicana Products, Inc.   I. Title.   II. Title:
Anthony T. Rossi.
BX6495.R678R67   1986   286'.13 [B]   86-27651
ISBN 0-8308-4999-8

17	16	15	14	13	12	11	10	9	8	7	6	5	4	3	2	1
99	98	97	96	95	94	93	92	91	90	89	88	87	86			

Foreword

During the past several years it's been my privilege to work with Anthony Rossi on several projects centered on missions, evangelism and the recording of Scripture for Third World countries. It's been thrilling to see a layman whose gifts and abilities have been yielded to God.

Anthony emigrated from Sicily to the United States and over the last six decades has become known as an astute and creative entrepreneur. His leadership in the manufacturing and marketing of Tropicana orange juice has established him among the successful in the business world.

His highest values have been reflected by a generous investment of himself and his resources in the kingdom of God. His personal love for God's Word and great burden to put it in the hands of those who have never heard it has been a personal challenge to me as well as to those around him. Another hallmark of Anthony's life has been the love and loyalty he has displayed to his family.

His story needed to be told and no one is better qualified to tell it than his wife, Sanna, who captures the humanness and the greatness of this man.

Cliff Barrows

Preface

Anthony T. Rossi at the age of 21 stood on the deck of a ship in 1921 entering New York Harbor from Italy. He called out, "There she is!" as he sighted the Statue of Liberty with the thrill only an emigrant can know arriving in America for the first time.

Although he came from a family of nine children, he was able to earn a dollar each ten-hour day, and within a few years owned taxicabs, a grocery store, farm, cafeteria, large restaurant and citrus packing plant. In 1947 he founded Tropicana Products, Inc., that became the largest fresh-chilled orange juice company in the world.

God guided Anthony Rossi to use Christian principles in his growing citrus industry. A commitment to top-quality products and to irreproachable honesty and fairness in dealing with his employees was paramount. He also desired fair dealings with those who were competitors in the orange juice business. This businessman daily communed with Jesus Christ, taking everything to the Lord in prayer and always giving God glory for the solution to difficult problems and the development of new ideas. All this, along with consistent reading of the Scriptures and obedience to God's leadership.

In the last ten years under Rossi's leadership, Tropicana doubled its profits every two and a half years and counted among the second five hundred industries in the United States showing the greatest progress, even heading that list.

Yet Anthony Rossi, recipient of so many honors and public acclaim, remained humble, approachable and ever thoughtful. He became a hero in the town of Bradenton, where twenty-eight hundred of its citizens held jobs at Tropicana. What was the background of this emigrant youth from Italy that would eventually see him as the founder, president and chairman of the board of Tropicana Products? Who without formal education was to move tons of fresh orange juice to the markets of America by ship as well as mile-long trains equipped with special refrigeration equipment that he developed. What was there in the childhood experiences and family background that equipped this giant of industry to such achievement and prepared him to be a Christian concerned for a world without Christ? To eventually found the Aurora Foundation that has generously given funding to assist Christian educational institutions, Christian missions and other charities? The following pages of this book will help the reader to understand how God takes a willing heart, such as Anthony Rossi's, and with it develops a servant-leader through a personal relationship with Jesus Christ.

It has been my privilege to know Anthony T. Rossi personally and to experience the warmth and Christian love of a man who has encouraged many people from all walks of life over the past 50 years. He recently celebrated his 86th birthday and his comment was, "I want to now go for 90 as my goal." The twinkle in his eye revealed a determination to do all he possibly could to make that goal that he might assist his fellow men and women for a while longer. May the model of Anthony T. Rossi be of great encouragement to each reader of this book.

John Kyle
InterVarsity Christian Fellowship

Acknowledgments

First of all, I am grateful to my husband, who, though he lives in a challenging present tense of activities, has told me of his boyhood in Italy and of his early life in America. He has patiently answered endless questions and has kept me on the track of accuracy and authenticity in this writing.

Large scrapbooks of the Tropicana story have been of great use as well. These were painstakingly done for "the Boss" by our mutual friend, Mr. Charles Johnson.

I am personally grateful for the help of Miss Virginia Jackson who conducts writing classes in the Continuing Education program offered by Manatee Community College. She encouraged me as I collected the contents bound between the covers of this book.

Also, I want to thank Georgia Aleppo, my husband's niece, for helping with details regarding family history and Italian spelling of places and things. The elder brother, Joseph T. Rossi has provided important Sicilian background data.

I am deeply indebted to my good friend, Miss Anne Isaacs, for her time and skill in typing the manuscript from handwritten notebooks. As my husband's personal accounts secretary, she has made time to do this work for me with cordial empathy and enthusiasm.

Finally, in addition to the friends who have encouraged this effort, I want to thank Mr. John Kyle of InterVarsity Christian Fellowship for his guidance and follow-through which brings forward a completed publication.

With such teamwork, these sketches have not relapsed into unfinished notes on a dusty shelf. Thank you to the many who have been most supportive of me.

Sanna Barlow Rossi

Introduction

"Have you seen this *Town and Country?*" A neighbor asked. It was the December issue of 1983. I noted the feature entitled "The Most Generous Living Americans" by Dan Rottenberg. As I paged through the article, my eyes focused on one heading, "Anthony T. Rossi, 82, Bradenton, Florida."

The paragraph was only ten lines, yet it compassed the core of Anthony Rossi's life goals. The summary read: "The Founder and former Chairman of Tropicana Products converted to Baptist faith after coming to the United States from Sicily; since then he has spent millions to further the work of Bible schools and missionary services—including the funding of a church in his native Sicily. His Aurora Foundation built the Bradenton Missionary Village, a one-hundred-acre, $10 million Florida community for retired missionaries." Thus, *Town and Country* had briefly summarized what this biography of Anthony Rossi is all about.

Yet it has been a special privilege to write between these lines a more personal sketch: not a comprehensive work, but a series of close-up vignettes to introduce a life that has inspired and encouraged many. It is like taking portraits of a person and seeing in them the most dominant characteristics like the hearty warmth and sincere smile of the man himself.

There have been those informal times with guests often in our home, or on other occasions, when Anthony Rossi has been persuaded to tell stories of his boyhood and later years as well. This has provided a vivid source of material, and beneath these window-views of his experiences, flows the inner-life motivations, the purpose, the goals. These are the secrets of indefatigable pursuit, running wide of discouragement, consistently confident that God's hand is upon him. To please God became his primary objective. Employing God-given talents to benefit others developed into a commitment to God to be useful for his work in the world.

It is this simplicity of seeking first to please God that has kept Anthony Rossi's long life remarkably shaped for outreach and blessing at home and worldwide.

This book ends too soon. There is so much more of the same pattern to share. But it is hoped the profiles chosen and placed in chronological order will reveal Anthony T. Rossi, a valuable friend whose verve and spirit do not slacken with years. Tomorrows hold bigger and greater things yet to accomplish.

Reminiscence

*B*RADENTON HERALD HEADLINES looked grim today. Large letters spelled out Tropicana's latest dilemma. As the biggest producer of fresh-chilled orange juice, the company faced tragic news. Florida's groves were blighted with spreading canker.

Anthony Rossi put the morning paper down and took his place at the breakfast table. His wife spoke first.

"Anthony, aren't you glad not to be at the helm of Tropicana now?"

"Why?" he countered.

"Well, they have increasing difficulty. Last month a freeze. Now the blight on the fruit. What a problem!"

"Problem?" His eyes, with keen vigor, expressed enough without words. "Not a problem, an opportunity!"

At this moment, other problems-cum-innovation marched out before them both in reverie.

"You remember that worst freeze?"

"Yes."

"And everybody wanted us to resort to reconstituted concentrate?"

"Right!"

"Well, our sales volume was $10 million a month. We led the citrus juice market. How could I fail people? How could I let quality suffer?"

"I remember." His wife knew he was thinking of the crisis that instigated another first for the company.

"That's when we made a processing plant on a barge. We took aboard Mexican oranges out of Tuxpan. We moved forward then. No retreat. Progress!"

"Mr. Tropicana, indeed."

His wife pondered the flash of recall. The paper had said, "The first floating factory of its kind. Sea-processed orange juice arrives Thursday." That date? It had been Monday, March 23, 1964. "Would you like to be back leading Tropicana?" she repeated. The question was automatic.

"No," Anthony replied decisively, "I don't want to return to Tropicana now. Though I would be glad to help, if I could. But today, just think of the opportunities we have with the Aurora and Bible Alliance Foundations! At Tropicana God enabled me to make money. Now he allows me the privilege of giving financial help where it counts most. No, I would not exchange opportunities today to impact missions for anything else in the world."

At the breakfast table, its south windows filled with the

front rose garden, Anthony Rossi lifted to his lips a tall glass of Tropicana orange juice. He tasted it, placing the glass again on the table. "Good. This is the Valencia season, when the juice is best."

Orange juice for breakfast at the Rossi's was a fixture.

"Anthony, when you were a boy in Sicily, did you ever dream of the wonderful things the future might hold?" His wife nudged him to reminisce.

"No, I never could have imagined building Tropicana; or even of coming alone to America with nothing. Can you believe I have lived in the United States, the greatest country in the world, for sixty-five years? Almost as old as you are!" He thought a bit, then added, "Now today, since Tropicana for me is past, I am so amazed at what God is doing at this time in Bible Alliance. Those New Testament albums to the blind and to the chaplains of the prisons—you should see the response we are getting every day. Terrific!"

Presently regular daily devotions resumed with the morning portion from Spurgeon's *Morning and Evening.* Next a reading from the Psalms followed by the through-the-Bible chapter marked for the day. To close this time with God's word, Anthony led in prayer: "And make this day a glorious day that we may do thy will and obey thy commandments—make us useful in thy service, we pray."

The pause that came next marked their reluctance to end this time together of focusing on the Lord.

"Nino, I was just wondering, thinking again of your boyhood in Sicily—can you tell me your very earliest childhood memory?"

He was thoughtful. The grandfather clock chimed Westminster bells. By now it was 8:30 A.M.

"Yes, I believe I can," he recalled, describing an episode

that reminded his wife of the man he was today—so often saying, "Don't worry, I'll take care."

The story itself was like opening tall wooden shutters upon an Italian garden of eight decades ago. The garden was bathed in summertime. The year was 1903, Messina, Sicily. Vesper bells were distant mellow reminders that the day was spent. Adolfo Rossi's front door opened to let a two-and-a-half-year-old boy out into the patio with his agile grandmother. Crossing it, they descended three steps into the garden. The rose bed was bordered with Italian tile. A yellow butterfly fluttering over the pink rose bush was too high for the little boy to reach. Face upturned, chestnut brown hair rippling in the breeze, he watched it—maybe it would swoop within his grasp. But the butterfly flew away. Birds twittered merrily in the nectarine tree close to the outer wall. Nonna and Nino could hear the hum of neighbors talking in the street beyond the wall. This was the time of day in Sicily that families emerged from their homes for a late afternoon stroll to visit with friends before nightfall. This surge of life was exciting as Messina revived from a sultry summer-day slump. Carriage wheels squeaked and horses thumped along the road outside.

The child took hold of a velvet-soft red rose blooming near the ground. He leaned over, smelling and caressing it.

Then, all of a sudden, he and Nonna saw a shiver in the violets bordering the roses. Down on his knees, Nino reached under the cover of green leaves, his chubby hand grabbing the prize. "Rana!"—a frog! Nonna marveled that the frog allowed the child to hold it. Nino studied toyish eyes turning left and right. Delighted with his new friend, he turned it over. Underneath, Rana was creamy white. The rest of its body was a camouflage of earth and leaves. Nino held it gently and stroked its cool kid-glove skin. Patting down a cozy spot for Rana in the violets, he carefully put it down again. The frog remained still, seemingly content, mesmerized.

"Come," Nonna called. "Ninutso, you must go up to bed. Say goodnight to Rana."

With one more pat for Rana, the bambino promised, "I'll see you in the morning. Stay right here until I come back."

Cheerfully he left with Nonna—happy to dream about that wonderful frog in the bed among the violets.

Next morning, Nino begged Nonna to open the garden door for him. Even before breakfast he must see his new playmate.

Quickly he went to the violet bed and found Rana's soft little room. But no frog! The little boy, with tears starting, searched the thick green leaves. The frog was nowhere to be found. Nino wept aloud.

Nonna's strong arms and soft words could not erase the keen sense of loss. And eighty-three years have not diminished it.

December 28, 1908

THE STURDY FOUR-YEAR-OLD reached up to drop a coin into the slit on the chicken's back. Nino loved this wonderful hen, always in place at the front entrance of the elegant department store owned by his parents. With his older brothers, Joe, Ricardo and Carlo, he was eager to see the hen lay chocolate eggs just for them. In 1904 Signor Adolfo Talamo-Rossi and his wife, Signora Rosaria La Via (called Sara), were prominent and affluent citizens in Messina. Adolfo Talamo-Rossi had been an only child as was also his wife. Their fathers had abandoned the home while each of them was very young. And since their own marriage, Adolfo's petite and charming mother, Anna, had shared their home. She was beloved by the children who called her Nonna, Italian for "grandmother." She was warm, cheery and a very helpful part of the household. Anna Machese Talamo-Rossi was deeply appreciated; her love and caring for the family enriched all.

Before 1908, however, the Talamo-Rossi's had suffered severe financial reverses. Sara's father, who had come to them to recuperate from an illness, later was granted the responsibility to buy imports for the store. This proved disastrous. He traveled in Europe and was so prodigal with funds that one day the Adolfo Rossi's woke up to find themselves bankrupt. Signor Talamo-Rossi, a singularly magnanimous person, was highly esteemed and loved in his hometown, as was also his wife. But it was difficult to bear such a setback. The store had to be dissolved, and they moved into simpler living quarters for their family. By now, Constantino had been born to join his four brothers, and in 1907, another brother, Alfredo, was born. Adolfo got a job as manager of the County Hospital. "Prefect," he was called.

Anthony (Nino to the family) recalled evenings by the light of kerosene lamps, when Mamá and Nonna would sit long into the night darning socks. No child of the Rossi's would be allowed to go barefoot on the street. They must wear shoes and socks always.

The little boys had soon forgotten about the hen that laid chocolate eggs and were caught up in other wonders. Besides their own innovative play (usually instigated by Nino) there were the miracles of electric light and the first automobile to be seen.

On the strand bordering the Messina harbor Nino and his brothers saw that horseless carriage for the first time. A relative, Signor Castalello, sat proudly at its steering wheel, and soon the vehicle rolled forward with its motor roaring. Nino tried to keep pace running alongside. As the car gained speed, he raced it—beside himself with excitement. But the monstrosity increased to a speed so great, the eight-year-old fell far behind. Who could match fifteen miles per hour?

Already the early 1900s promised a spectacular century ahead. Then, however, no one could have imagined going to the moon.

Nevertheless, just three days before 1908 closed, an event occurred that totally changed the antique sea ports of Messina in Sicily and Reggio across the straits.

Sicily's northernmost seaport faces Italy's boot, five miles across the Straits of Messina. It fronts the sea by a narrow brick-paved street called Via Victor Emmanuele. Behind the street stretched a wall of buildings, bastions against the narrow border of the quay. Sailboats and merchant ships anchored near the ornate Fountain of Neptune. In the deep silence of the early morning, these were but solid shadows. The night was hushed. The city of about 100,000 settled into the cliffs and crevices of Sicily's mountainous shores.

Opposite Messina on Italy's south coast spread the city of Reggio Calabria with its string of villages from heel to toe. St. Paul had passed by Messina when he disembarked at Reggio in the first century. The place was old and ever a prize for sight-seers.

The metropolis of Messina fitted thickly into the hills. Level places were few, with large wall-to-wall buildings and closed-in streets too narrow for horse-drawn carriages to pass. Here and there in the suburbs single houses nestled among olive and citrus groves. Grape vineyards terraced the steep slopes. Some embankments were covered in prickly pear cacti.

The city boasted many famous cathedrals, all built in ancient brick and adobe as was the architecture everywhere. Arched gates and doors as well as the interiors were carved and painted by Italy's many renowned artists: Montorasoli, Batista Mazzola, Antonella de Messina and others. Messina was proud of these. Visitors would not miss seeing them.

Most of the people lived in three- or four-storied condominiums with wide entrances and stairways. Each apartment was owned by the family using it. The Talamo-Rossi's slept that night in their third-floor home set snugly against a mountain buttress. Sara and Adolfo Rossi with their children, all boys at this date, were warmly tucked under blankets. The night was cold. A light rain was falling. Joe, the eldest at about fourteen, had stayed home that night instead of Ricardo. At the last minute Ricardo, twelve, had persuaded Joe to let him be the one to attend to an ill relative, a professor who lived several narrow streets away. But Carlo, ten, and Anthony, eight, were home together; also the baby Constantino who was only three, an infant Alfredo and the paternal grandmother, Nonna Annetta.

All was quiet, normal. Another night, like a hundred thousand before, passed over the beautiful city.

At about 5:00 A.M., an unusual disquietude among animals broke the stillness. In the distance cattle began to low; cocks shrieked, dogs howled and whimpered. In the Rossi home, a caged bird frantically fluttered against the bars, chirping wildly. Suddenly it struck—*Torramodo*—Earthquake—a rolling, shivering, violent shaking underneath.

The Rossi's sprang from their beds. Adolfo and Sara gathered their boys and Nonna, and propelled them down the two swaying stairways. Down, down, midst the roar and the trembling. They reeled toward the outside door. Adolfo had trouble opening the door. Precious seconds passed. Then, just as he finally opened the door and as they huddled together under the arch of the massive entrance, the third tremor rolled beneath them, shook them like a sieve leveling sand castles back into dust. The whole edifice crumbled. Thunderous *rumore*. The front walls fell outward to the street. Gas fires flared in Palazzo Casibile and other places, licking into garish light the predawn sky. Messina was devastated, crumbled in moments into ruin. The same was true of Reggio and villages across the Straits of Messina.

Mingled with the terror of shattering timbers and mortarpowder, the family could hear the cries of victims trapped in the debris. Screams sounded above the disintegrating buildings. Moaning, wailing, filled the cold darkness. Ten or twenty minutes crept passed while the Rossis trembled underneath the intact arch that saved them. With the first light of day, they saw more clearly the stark nightmare around them.

Adolfo saw a woman staggering over debris nearby. She had no clothes. He scrambled to throw a blanket around her. Nino and his brothers were transfixed with horror. Had the world come to an end? Was this everywhere?

Venturing out at last, the Rossi parents headed their family toward a vacant lot near Via San Marino. Later they went for the dry river bed as a safer escape route from the destroyed city. They could see no edifice left standing. In agony Nino watched a small boy about his own size struggling to carry on his bowed back the body of his dead brother.

Adolfo, Sara, Nonna, and their five children trudged doggedly along the dry channel toward Aunt Emelia's place in the country. Maybe, they hoped, her home had not fallen. They found Aunt Emelia outside her house. Somewhat askew, it still stood, but she dared not stay indoors while every five minutes the earth trembled. They crowded together, stiff with shock and incredulity. Nino felt hungry. He and his brothers tried out the lemons on Aunt Emelia's tree, but their acidity only increased the craving for real food.

The disaster to Messina had been total. Around eighty thousand people perished. Tragically, one of those was the Rossi's son, beautiful Ricardo—the only one whose brown hair curled so beautifully over his head. He was a victim along with the professor's wife. Miraculously, the sick professor, confined to his bed, fell three floors to the ground, yet was spared injury of any kind.

After three days, the first rescue ship from the outside world arrived at the ruined port. It was a large Russian vessel. Among the first hundred refugees climbing aboard were the Rossi's. Immediately they received bread and butter to eat. Nino could not remember ever tasting food so good. For three days he and his family had fasted.

The welcome ship carried them also to safety and shelter. They sailed along the Sicilian coast to the unharmed port of Syracuse. There they found residence in a hotel until hastily constructed prefabricated barracks provided them with temporary accommodations.

In Syracuse that one year and a half, Nino often thought about Judgment Day. Looking up into Sicily's azure sky he longed to know more about God. *I hope I go to heaven when I die! That is where Ricardo is. He was so good. I'm a rascal, but I love God and also want to live my life to please him.*

Messina's citizens determined to rebuild a better city, no matter how long it would take. For one of the Rossi family in Syracuse a particular day would come and go, a day in his life destined to make a significant difference. But at the crossroads on this day, Nino, quite by accident, made the choice himself. Today in 1986, remembering, he would say as he so often does, "God loves me. And all he does is for my own good."

An Important
Coincidence

T HE EARLY MORNING TRAIN whistle blew a receding
lonesome wail. In a small makeshift barracks, the Rossi boys
wakened. Slowly they realized that Papá with Mamá were on
that train departing Syracuse for Messina. The Signores Talamo-Rossi had gone for the day, hoping to be able to sell
property in Messina and to ascertain progress there in the
struggle to reconstruct the city. They would return to Syracuse in the evening.

Anna, the paternal grandmother, was in charge. The
grandsons loved her. She anticipated the usual agenda for
this summer day. Breakfast was simple—milk warmed with
a bit of Italian coffee and a brioche (soft roll). By the time

breakfast was over, an occasional horse and carriage rumbled along the cobblestone street. The usual morning sounds of the city.

Nonna presided over the house, keeping the small quarters neat, the dishes done, the clothing washed. She gave special attention to the youngest, Constantino and Alfredo. Carlo and Joe were old enough to entertain themselves and do some chores. And Anthony, she always kept on eye on him. The eight-year-old with dimpled smile and fun-filled large gray eyes was often endearingly called Ninutso by Nonna. Nino could be roguish without warning and often amused his brothers with the originality of his pranks.

Nonna did recall today a rumor that had circulated. English friends from Britain were working to relieve the plight of refugees from Messina's earthquake. Two ladies from England were interested in the barracks people of Syracuse. They were looking for junior-age children eligible for boarding school in central or northern Italy. Anthony Talamo-Rossi was one of the names on their list. First must come the exploratory interview. Their visit was to be unannounced.

The summer day grew into afternoon. Lunch dishes had just been put away clean. Carlo and Joe were first to see the approach of a horse-drawn carriage rattling up to the barracks' gate.

"They are coming to see us!" they shouted. And Nonna agreed when two important-looking ladies descended from their carriage and approached the door. Nonna opened the door to greet them graciously, though she was cautious.

She had not noticed Nino's absence as the older brothers stood by at a discreet distance. Nino, however, by some unexplainable impulse, had picked up the partly used bottle of dinner wine and imbibed a quantity of it, finishing the whole bottle. He was quite unprepared for the sensation that followed—one so unpleasant and vivid that he would forever begrudge alcoholic beverages. A warm excitement pervaded his body. He began to yell. The room whirled and swung back and forth around him. Flopping on his cot, he was seized by an emotion of intense hostility.

This was the Anthony Rossi the proper ladies were to meet. When Nonna brought the visitors to Nino, she was alarmed to see a red-faced, glazed-eyed little boy, wild, tantrum-prone and utterly incoherent.

Politely, the ladies withdrew as Nino watched their witchy faces grimace and nod. He wanted to fight them too.

"Thank you very much, Signora Rossi, we must be on our way now."

As the carriage pulled away, Nonna was choked with perplexity. Then she noticed on the kitchen table the empty wine bottle. By the time she composed herself to check on the boy, he was sound asleep, clenched fists relaxed, light brown hair tousled. Yet the flushed face of her rascal-boy was angelic in slumber.

Two or three hours passed before he woke up, finally sober.

"I'm sorry Nonna. I won't drink wine again. I don't like it. I hate it."

"Fine," said Nonna.

"When will my parents be back?"

"In a little while." Nonna looked at the clock. "In two hours, maybe."

"Are you going to tell Papá?" Nino was apprehensive.

"Well, Ninutso, I will have to report to him, but let me tell you a secret. If you go to bed right after supper, Papá will find you asleep when he comes back. You know he will never spank you when you are sleeping."

The word was to the wise. The youngster forfeited all the fun of greeting his parents and hearing news of Messina. When they got home, he was safely in bed, eyes shut tight in pretended sleep.

Carlo and Joe discussed the big event of the day with much relief. "We are certainly glad our Nino will not be taken away from us to boarding school. We are happy!"

Sure enough, as the hat-and-glove ladies had bounced away, their pencils decidedly scratched out the name of Anthony Talamo-Rossi from Messina, Sicily. Another plan of God had prevailed. And by early 1910 the Rossi family were packing up to return again to Messina. It was a ruins still, yet they believed in its future. They left Syracuse with hope warming their hearts.

Nonna's Rosary

AFTER THE YEAR AND A HALF in Syracuse, the Talamo-Rossis were back in Messina to see and hear the labored recovery of the great city. From the the debris, new avenues and streets followed an orderly plan and were wide, often paved with igneous rock which had spewed from the earthquake itself. Buildings gradually came up again, well-constructed and designed for endurance.

In 1910, when Anthony was still nine years old, the Rossis settled again in a housing makeshift of extensive barracks put up with lumber from the United States of America. Temporary and crowded, this situation was of no inconvenience to the Rossi boys. In fact, they delighted in the proximity of others their own age. Life for them was never uneventful. They loved living in Villa Virgini Elena.

And there was always a small baby in the Rossi home. With Constantino old enough to walk and talk, Alfredo now occupied the cradle and Nino grew up loving each newcomer in the home. Family ties were strong. Though always proud of his older brothers, Joe and Carlo, he went his own way in play adventures and had his preference of playmates of whom he was noticeably the leader.

One late afternoon, Nino came in earlier than usual from play. He sat down on a low stool at his grandmother's feet. His eyes studied her face. He watched as she took out her rosary. Did Nonna know God? With large questioning eyes Nino asked, "Nonna, may I think about God with you?"

"Why yes, Ninutso, we can do the rosary together."

Nonna Annetta touched a bead. "Santa Maria," she said. And the boy responded excitedly.

"Ora pro nobis," Nonna continued with the next bead. "Santa de Genori."

"Ora pro nobis," the boy sat still, serious about this tryst with God.

"Santa Virgo Virgini," softly Nonna spoke. And Nino breathed the response. "Ora pro nobis."

Would they go through the entire rosary? Perhaps. Nino could not usually sit still for so long, but now he was spellbound by the liturgy.

Ever since that catastrophic earthquake a year and a half ago, he had wondered about heaven. The trauma of witnessing a whole city crumble in minutes, then the wailing, the horror, the rain —all this shocked him into understanding the fragility of life. How he missed his brother, Ricardo! For some reason, God had spared Nino with the rest of his family as they huddled beneath the solid arch that held when the rest of the building collapsed.

Since then, Nino longed to find God, to come close to him. He never missed going to church on Sunday. And gladly took up the charge as altar boy. The priest knew he could count on this one, Anthony Rossi, to come on time and without fail, and to perform his duty conscientiously. Yet the question still troubled Nino. Sometimes that profound concern would surface. "How can I know I am going to heaven when I die?"

A grownup heard Nino ask this question aloud and he volunteered an answer. "Just be careful to say, every morning and every evening, three Ave Marias, three Lord's Prayers, three Credos, and three Virgin Marys. Don't miss a morning or evening for seven years. Then you will go to heaven when you die."

Nino resolved to do these prayers every night and every morning. Sometimes, however, after an exhausting day, he fell asleep in the midst of reciting all of them. Next morning, recalling his omissions, he disciplined himself by repeating the prayers seven times around. This was to make up for the last night's lapse. (This he did for seven years. Then added seven more to be sure of heaven.)

Now Nino sat quietly, intent on repeating the rosary with Nonna. "Santa Lucia, ora pro nobis."

At the final "Ora pro nobis," Nonna paused and stood to her feet. Nino instantly helped her from her chair. Then, taking his sunny face into her two hands, she kissed him on both cheeks.

"*Grazia,* Ninutso." Nonna perceived that this superactive child, often dubbed *birbanti* (rascal), had a tender heart for God. She could not measure, however, the intensity of his desire to know God and to please him.

"Some day I want to build a chapel with a rose garden in front. Or, maybe some day I can go to another country and be a missionary. We have relatives who went to Brazil to serve God. I want to do something, be something for God." These were thoughts unuttered but persistent within.

The next minute the angel, Nino, changed into the nine-year-old all-boy activist again. Carlo and Joe came up to him. "Mamá says we are to wash up for supper. And Nino, where were you today? You were not in school."

The question received no answer—only an inscrutable twinkle in the rascal-boy's intelligent eyes.

The Other Side
of Sicily?

WINTER ALWAYS MEANT heavier clothes and the unrelenting threat of school. School demanded sitting still for the body and intolerable repetition to shackle the mind. To Nino school was an ordeal of boredom. Yet, once in awhile, he could be counted present to swiftly learn his alphabet, grammar, numbers, and, on his own, to pick up the arias of Italian operas, along with the popular songs of the 1910s. Nino was forever singing. At this time in early 1911, he was 10 years old.

"Today," he mused, "I really will go to school."

Then Papá approached his boy, Anthony, and counseled him. "Son, this afternoon I want you to go to school. Get a good start. You know it is on Via San Martino five miles from where we are in Villagie Virgine Elena. Here is ten cents for your recess. Be a good boy now. *Arrivederci.*"

Papá persuaded him so kindly. "I will go," he resolved. He had gone about a block when Giovanne appeared. "Giovanne, where have you been?"

"Oh," shrugged the suntanned ten-year-old, "Out on a sailing boat with my father, fishing. He wants me to go with him again. But I wish I didn't have to go."

"Well," Nino lowered his voice, "I don't really want to go to school either. I've got an idea!"

"What?"

"Let's go over to the other side of Sicily. We can find out what it's like over there!"

The little boys turned away from the direction of the school. "We'll need more money." Nino looked at his ten cents. "I know, the Professor, our cousin. He has some gold fish. Cadunio wants to buy some gold fish."

To the professor's gold-fish pool they headed with a can in hand. Gold fish they took to Cadunio. But he could only pay for half of them. The boys hid the remainder in the can underneath one of the barracks' houses where Giovanne's family also stayed.

With evening coming on, Nino and Giovanne hid themselves in a broom closet off the circular conference room at the barracks. After a while the Rossi family whistle reached out for Nino—clear, insistent, pleading, "me do sooo fa." Older brothers Joe and Carlo were searching. "We can't find Nino," they wailed. "If you see him, anybody, please bring him home, me do sooo fa."

The boys huddled, breathing carefully, sitting very still for a long, long time. Silence at last snuffed out the "me do sooo fa."

"Let's hurry," Nino whispered. They scurried out of the closet to the back of the barracks' rows of two-bedroom flats. Each flat had separate kitchen quarters. Picking a kitchen three sections down from his own, Nino cautiously opened the screen door and sneaked inside. He found a candle, a cooking pot, some sugar, some coffee. The floor squeaked.

"Kees, Kees!" the signora indoors thought he was a cat!

Out again, Nino with Giovanne watching, crept over to the next kitchen shack to get another candle, more sugar, and coffee. Then to a third. Enough.

Back into the broom closet with their loot, they waited. Would daylight never come?

The small boys asleep dreamed of a fabulous journey over Sicilian mountains to exciting places yet to see.

In the barracks, early morning came with startling discoveries for three signores. "Aye, aye! Someone has robbed my coffee! No sugar. My husband must have breakfast before he goes to work! Can you lend me," to a neighbor, "a little coffee, sugar?"

"Aye, aye, mine is gone too!"

"And mine—mine too," cried the third signora. Dawn was still pearl gray. The boys were wide awake. With an old grocery list wrinkled in his fist, Nino emerged with Giovanne. They were out the barracks's gate and into the street. Fresh air! They could see the grocery store a block away.

"With our list, we'll get the food we need, and then—"

Shouts came from behind them. "Nino, Nino, there he is!" Nino ran as fast as he could, but the larger boys, friends of his brothers, tackled him and brought him down. Each took an arm and leg. The four hauled him ignobly to his home and the waiting chastisement.

Brother Joe took his clothes away and tied him down in

his bed. "By this, you will be kept from Papá's punishing you!" he explained.

Then came the inevitable inquisition. "The gold fish! Where are the professor's gold fish?"

Nino told all. "Cadunio bought half. Here's the money. The others are in a can under Signora Natalia's kitchen—coffee, sugar, candles, pot." All these were also returned.

Miserably bound to his bed, Nino felt the weight of reality as that vision of Sicily's other side vanished away.

The Washwoman's
Story

TWO OR THREE DAYS PASSED. Nino, biting his lip to keep from crying, watched his Nonna Annetta try to untie the strings of cloth binding him to his bed. "Nino," Nonna looked straight into his eyes, her dark brown eyes full of loving concern, "why did you and Giovanne try to run away?" At last free, the boy, almost as tall as his tiny grand-mother, explained.

"Well, Nonna, you see, Giovanne didn't want to go away again on a fishing trip. We both thought it would be great to hike over to see the other side of Sicily!" Excitement flushed his cheeks, and his gray eyes were laughing. Life was such glorious fun!

Nonna, glad to have freed Nino from the bedpost, reached out to him. With a pent-up sob of relief, he threw his arms around her and thanked her.

"Molta Grazia."

"Ninutso," Nonna said earnestly. "Remember, he who loves you makes you cry. He who hates you makes you laugh."

Clothed now in only his undergarments and shoes, Nino thought about this new meaning to his present disciplining—house bound.

Suddenly a clatter and bang at the back door and hearty *"Buon giuorno"* announced the buxom washwoman. Her cheeks rosy with health and cheer, she greeted them. *"Come sta, Signora, come stai, Nino?"*

"Enter, enter," Nonna insisted. Then Nino saw the door shut again on a vibrant, sunny morning. Into that outside he was not allowed to go.

"The clothes for washing?"

"Yes, yes, Donna, but first sit down." And Nonna placed demitasse cups of Italian coffee on the kitchen table. Both sat down to visit a bit before listing the laundry items. The washing had to be done at a neighbor's farmhouse where there was a *gebbia*, or irrigation pool, and plenty of water.

"What to do?" Nino was restive and quickly forgotten by the women conversing at the table. "Mamá will be making pasta-fajoli for lunch today—I smell it cooking—onions and tomato with the beans already bubbling on the stove. Spaghetti goes in the last few minutes before serving. Mamá is busy too." But, Nino sighed, it would be three hours, long hours, before lunchtime. This yummy pasta was a favorite dish for the Rossis, and very inexpensive too. They would be eight at the table, and all with good appetites.

"Maybe Nonna will let me help her gather up the linens and towels for the wash?" Just then, a shrill whistle pierced the open window near the wall separating the barracks from the street. Nino ran and leaned out to look across the wall. Lello and Alfonso in the street beckoned vigorously. "Nino, come, come with us!"

"Just a minute!" Nino disappeared. His clothes were hidden. But he found a coat of his father's, hurriedly put it on and returned to the window. Scrambling out, he found a place on the wall where the ground below was sloped enough to allow him to jump from the wall. He made the jump safely.

The boys were off like the wind, and as free. Heading across a field and to a fence easy to climb over, they came to the orchard of the very farmer whose water supply was made available to the washwoman.

Nino was first to find a tree loaded with ripening pears. Zipping up it, the youngsters had found a real prize. Nino balanced in a fork of limbs and reached up for a golden pear.

But he was interrupted. The farmer had spotted the boys, and he shouted frantically. Others joined in the hue and cry, *"Birbanti!"* (rascal). The farmer recognized the son of Adolfo Talamo-Rossi and screamed. "It is the prefetto's son, the prefetto's son!"

Nino skidded to the ground and was on the run before his accomplices could get out of the tree. Across the farmer's orchard, over a fence, through the pasture, to the road, to the wall, and up it to the window, still open. Inside, whisking his father's coat out of sight, Nino stood nonchalantly as before, wearing the limited clothing allowed him—only his underwear.

"*Ciao*, Nino!" said the washwoman as she left with her bundle of laundry. "Be a good boy."

However, when the Donna appeared at the farmer's house and put down her clothes, she was bombarded with the words. "The prefetto's son! Stealing pears. *Birbanti.*"

"No, no!" She declared indignantly, "You are wrong. The boy is kept at home, not even properly dressed to go out. He was there when I came in this morning, and I told him good-bye when I left. It could not have been the prefetto's son."

The farmer, still angry, abruptly dismissed the laundress from his gebbia. She would have to find another water supply for the Talamo-Rossi clothes.

The news about the pear tree spread—a new spice of gossip to liven an ordinary day. Nonna even heard of the accusation. Turning to Nino as he stood beside her in the kitchen, she put her arm around his shoulder. "Now, see, Nino, you have such a reputation. *Birbanti.* Even when you are innocent people suspect you. Remember, 'He who hates you makes you laugh. He who loves you makes you cry.' Nonna always loves you, Ninutso."

A Day at School

WATCH, CARLO, IT'S SIMPLE." Nino took a thick short piece of bamboo and placed a hunk of cheese on one end. "This is the way to catch a mouse." He then placed a pot upside down over the stick so that the pot rested on the outside end of it. Inside the pot was the cheese. The rim of the pot had to balance on the very edge of the stick. "Now, see!" Nino was sure Carlo could guess the trick.

"I'll see if you catch a mouse," Carlo said skeptically.

Some time later, when Nino went out the back door to inspect his trap, it had sprung!

The pot was now flat on the ground. "Carlo, Carlo, we have a mouse! The mouse went under the pot and when he touched the cheese, the pot slipped off the edge of the stick. Now he is inside."

They carefully lifted the pot. Two mice! Nino caught them in a paper bag. Nino jovially announced, "Now it is time to go to school."

"You! Go to school? Early?" Carlo was not the only one to be surprised. Anthony did get to his classroom ahead of time. Nobody noticed when he went first to the teacher's desk or that he carried a paper bag.

Class began, as usual, with recitation.

"Anthony Rossi, will you please repeat the poem for today?"

The boy answered humbly, "I'm sorry, I do not know it.' Nino watched another child stand to his feet and recite the poem. As soon as Andrea sat down, Nino's hand shot up. "I know it now." But the teacher was unconvinced.

"You told me, Anthony, that you could not say the poem."

"I do know it now." And he stood to repeat the poem perfectly, having heard it only once.

"How encouraging this would be to his parents," the teacher mused. "I must tell them about it."

In the course of the afternoon, the teacher opened her desk drawer. Out sprang two fuzzy mice, landing right in her lap! Pandemonium in the classroom was all that Nino had hoped it could be!

Returning home that day, Anthony Rossi carried a note from the teacher to his father. Something else to think about was that impending spanking. "I loved the arithmetic session," he remembered a highlight of the day. "Kept ahead of the teacher. She was too slow. But now I know what's coming. Papá spanks me every day. I am such a rascal."

The Prefetto's Garden

AT FOUR O'CLOCK IN THE morning, Anthony was wide awake. Would daylight never come? He could hardly wait. Watching the mysterious moving gray of predawn, he yearned for morning. Gradually the dark tweed elfin air flattened and turned lighter, then opalescent. When finally the first pink of morning smiled at his window, he was up and into work clothes and old shoes, out the back door into the yard to work. He knew what he would do with that one-acre space now littered with earthquake debris.

Already he had thought through how to build the garden. He fell to the task undaunted by those heavy chunks of broken brick and rock. Tugging and hauling them one at a time, he pitched them to the side.

The Rossi home by 1911 was within the ten-acre hospital compound. Their house was adequate for an expanding family and secure within the walls of the hospital area where the convent and a church had been built, along with the large Ospedale Piemonte of which Anthony's father was manager or prefetto.

The rubble-heaped yard beside his home was the focus of Nino's intense concern. "What I will do," he told the eighty-year-old hospital compound gardener, Santo Bombaci, "is clear off a line of the land this wide, pacing a six-foot width. Then, Don Santo, I will show you what I will do. Just watch." The gardener provided flowers for the hospital but was not able to work hard now. He was bent over so that his face was toward the earth he so loved and cultivated. He and the child-gardener were of one heart. He would stick with Nino to guide and encourage him and to watch his ambitious dream, if possible, materialize.

Muscular and strong for his eleven years, Nino did not tire or tolerate discouraging observations. True, it was a task for a bulldozer, not a small boy, but his zeal was fierce, absorbing mind and body. No day was ever long enough, no night too short.

At seven the next morning, he took a quick break, coffee-milk with a brioche for breakfast. Then Nino was back again to tackle the debris. In his vision the place was already the garden of the prefetto.

First the acre plot must be covered in good soil instead of the rubble. After finally clearing one six-foot-wide lane, Nino took pick and shovel and began to dig three feet of sod out of the cleared stretch. He was careful to pitch all the dirt to the side. "Don Santo, soon I'll have the first trench done. You'll see."

As Santo sat nearby on a hunk of rock, watching, Nino noticed that the old man's pipe was empty. He remembered cigar butts he had collected. Nobody else knew where they were. He ran quickly to fetch them. Taking Santo's pipe, Nino carefully emptied the unused tobacco into it until the bowl was full. Pressing it down, he handed it to his friend, a constant companion these days.

"Now, Don Santo, you can smoke. And let's think where to buy the best seeds for the garden," Nino urged. "I want to raise all the vegetables we use in our home. This garden must be the best!" As the boy worked, he and the kind old man would talk for hours of the hows and whys of growing a great variety of vegetables and fruit trees. "We want nectarine trees, peaches and, of course, fig trees. Also, I have a good walnut seed, Don Santo. Will you show me how deep to plant it. I hope it will grow!" (And it did, marking his garden spot for years to come.)

When the first length of trench was done, the boy dragged into it all the debris he had piled to the side, and then shovelled the rich bank of dirt over it. This he leveled off so that a smooth swath of ground, measuring the length of the yard, became the first strip of prepared soil. The garden had begun. But only the beginning.

Too soon the days passed. Nino, bathed and dressed for dinner, would sit at the long table with his family. *"Buon appetito!"* spoke to his mood. Once he leaned toward his plate too eager for that first bite of pasta.

"No, Ninsuto," instructed Papá gently. "Remember, the mouth does not seek the fork. The fork must seek the mouth."

Table manners were important to the Talamo-Rossi family. Adolfo Talamo-Rossi himself had a hobby of cooking gourmet food. Often in the evenings Nino observed him in the kitchen, creating delicious entrees for the table.

But Papá was always careful not to season food with pepper or strong spices. "There's pepper on the table," Papá announced. "But there is no pepper in the food because Nino's tongue is too sensitive. No pepper in Nino's food."

Anthony appreciated this special consideration and mused upon the coincidence that since his busy garden building had begun, there had been no spankings, not even once, for days and days. Now magnificently obsessed with gardening and Santo's blessing, Nino had forgotten the barracks of Villagio Virgini Elena and the many times of mischief-making. He was much too busy now to remember those faraway things.

After many more months of unflagging labor in company with Don Santo, the plot of ground was finally, and perfectly, ready for planting. Nino had even irrigated it with criss-crossing trenches as Santo directed. Next came the much-looked-for days of planting. Santo brought in the seeds they wanted: eggplant, cauliflower, artichoke, broccoli, carrot, zucchini, celery, lettuce, escarole, endive, basilica, parsley, garlic, onion and much more. Such a variety, and each to be planted according to its own specifications.

Santo found the onion plants Nino especially wanted. And the young gardener had so many that the idea of going into business for himself tempted him. Nino planted several rows of the onion shoots along the entire length of one end of the garden. When they reached a certain maturity, he pulled them up and bunched them together. These he took to a young friend and bargained with him.

"If you will take these down there to the bridge where the farmers bring in their fresh produce, you can sell these for me and I will give you a percentage of the profit!"

"*Justo!*" The boy agreed. Nino watched him from a distance. Selling onions began a profitable business. However, Nino knew his father would not approve of the prefetto's son selling onions! And sure enough, one day the prefetto discovered his son's latest interest. Visitors to the hospital patients remarked about the quantity of onions in the prefetto's garden.

"Oh, my son's onions. Take all you want. Help yourselves. What can we do with so many?" Nino's father, always a giving person, was today generosity itself.

And Nino saw the demise of his onion business. He heard his father, whisper, "Would he sell the onions? My son— never!"

But the garden! *Mirabille!* For the larger Rossi family was now Carlo, Anthony, Constantino, Alfredo and baby Salvatore, along with their parents and grandmother. (Joe had gone away to nautical preparatory school.) The garden produced enormous cauliflower and broccoli. Romaine lettuce was picked tender-sweet for *ensaladas* deluxe. Daily Nino brought vegetables and fruit to the kitchen, the abundance shared also with friends. His garden became known as the best in town. So much *"sul la tavola, O joya."*

At Messina's Port

THE SUMMERTIME AFTERNOON was sunny. Nino's garden flourished, but today it needed little attention. But the waterfront was, as always, magnetizing. At age thirteen, Nino could find exciting things to do at the port. Back at home, he thought with pleasure, the baby in the family was, at last, a little girl, Elvira. She was one year old this August 15, 1913. "And Constantino helped me this morning to select vegetables for the table." Nino's thoughts were happy as he approached the water's edge today. There at the wharf he might volunteer to help some passengers across from the shore at Messina to the Mole, that slip of land where Messina's Lady of the Harbor welcomed visitors much like America's Statue of Liberty. Rowing was fun, mainly because it was helpful work, serving people. Nino refused to take pay for this. It would be about ten cents a trip, but the boat owner always treated him with fresh fruits from the market—nectarines, the sweetest in the world, or fresh figs and peaches. But no rowing would he choose this afternoon. Nor would he be watching the expertise of swordfishing. Sometimes he had done this, boarding a larger fishing boat going out farther into the Straits. That was fascinating—to see a boy climb to the mast of the sailboat in order to spot the swordfish when it might surface. With a sight of the swordfish he would shout, pointing directly to it. A man at the front of the boat then threw his spear at the fish. If he was accurate, a great shout of applause rewarded his skill. But, oh, if he missed, derision and scorn pelted him. A chance to watch this sport at close range was a rare adventure. Swordfish was often a delicacy at the Rossi table. Papá could make delicious swordfish rollups on a skewer to be served with gourmet sauce. *"Uttimo gusto."*

But now, however, Nino chose to try his own fishing line at the wharf. He found an empty barge jutting into the water at one end. He climbed to the top of the stern and began to cast his line for fish. No success. The minutes slowly floated away with the tide beneath the barge. He kept casting out the line farther and farther. At last, he leaned out, stretching to the limit to cast his line the greatest length yet. Then, suddenly too far over the edge for balance, Nino toppled off the barge. "Oopla!" A flat splash and under the water he went. It was deep enough to protect him from injury. Corking up, blubbering, Nino saw his rod and line float out, lost forever to the wide blue Mediterranean. The current of the Straits of Messina were swift. Drenched with salt water, Nino stood on the sand looking at his clothes.

"The salt water will rot them," he regretted. "And I don't have a lot of clothes, because there are so many of us for Mamá and Papá to care for."

He turned from the water and looked toward the fish and fruit market opposite. It was called the Pescaria, an area fenced by slender iron posts with a wide gate. The place was popular. Many people were bargaining at the market. In the midst of this busy square was a three-foot-high cylindrical fountain where fresh water from the shadowing mountain flowed over its circular ledge and into a shallow pool.

Nino made a dash for the splashing fountain. He sat down on the ledge around its base. Fresh, cool water now thoroughly rinsed away all the salt water from his clothes. In about fifteen minutes, he emerged from the fountain, dripping until the warm Sicilian sun dried his clothes so that he could walk home.

Arriving home in time for supper, Nino, neat as all the rest, sat in his place at the dining table.

"Nino, what did you do today?" piped Constantino, called Tino by the family.

"Went fishing. Didn't catch anything." And nobody guessed the rest of the story. Nino knew his clothing would not be spoiled because of salt water even though he had brought no fish home for the family dinner.

Gelato

IT WAS A GALA DAY FOR THE Talamo-Rossis late in 1914. For on October 31, another baby had been born, another girl. Her name was Teresa. Vivacious little Elvira was only two years old.

Nino was especially happy because his mother was so glad. At last the family seemed complete with two little girls. Their six brothers rejoiced with their parents. Nino especially adored Mamá. "She is beautiful. Tall, slender, so much depth in her dark eyes. I believe baby Teresa looks a little like Mamá," he concluded after a long look at two-month-old Teresa in her crib. His mother had a natural elegance about her—those perfect patrician features and her long brown hair done up neatly in a large bun at the back of her neck.

Nino thought today his mother looked a little pale, but she seemed well. What a warm vivacious hostess she was. "Mamá doesn't get to go to church with me," Nino mused. "But she prays a lot. She is always too busy taking care of all of us. Mamá loves us, especially me. I see her working on my socks and clothes almost every evening. She and Nonna sit up late, long after we children have gone to sleep, while Papá attends a hospital board meeting or is busy at his office." Nino grew up knowing his mother's priority was her home—her children, her husband and other family members like beloved Annetta Machese. Her husband's mother was a very dear part of her life, like her own mother in fact. Today, the big day of fiesta for baby Teresa, Nonna was taking full charge of the baby, so that Sara could welcome the many guests who were coming. Nino, too, had the knack of being helpful in practical ways, and family and friends tended to gravitate to him. Perhaps because happiness is catching, and that wonderful smile cheered everyone.

Just now, Nino was in the kitchen where he watched closely as Papá took charge. Like an artist Papá prepared some of the specialties for baby Teresa's christening celebration.

Many relatives and close friends would be arriving soon to celebrate this baby's baptism. Aunt Elvira, Sara's great aunt, was even now on her way, taking the trolley from Giampilieri. Possibly it was Carlo who was assigned to meet her and bring her to the house. Constantine had already announced the approach of others. Sara was at the front door with a cordial welcome. They were Adolfo's great aunts this time. Aunt Teresa, in her nun's vestments, they called

Zia Teresa la Monica. She had come from the convent tucked into a niche in the hills that embraced the city. Ironically, Zia Emelia la Protestante came next. The only Protestant in the family connection, the older boys remembered her hospitality on that dreadful day of the earthquake. And often her home was home to Joe who had stayed with his Zia Emelia many times. She too had come several miles to reach her great nephew's place within the walled compound of the county hospital. Like Zia la Monica for whom the baby was named, Zia Emelia was received with sincere love and respect. Today was for family. And they were gathering about making things ring with laughter, affection and joy. Though in December, Sicilian weather was mild. But homes were not heated, and wearing warm clothes adjusted everyone to the cooler season of the year.

Papá, still in the kitchen, had added the exact amount of red wine to the flour which had been precisely weighed. He began to roll the kneaded lump into a paper-thin sheet of dough. Then he used a wide cutter to make the mauve-colored circles of pastry known as cannoli. Nino, now fourteen years old, was alert to any activity that became a learning experience. He saw Papá fold the thin pastry over a short bamboo stick, just right to drop into the bubbling light oil in a deep frying pan on the stove.

"May I help, Papá?"

"Of course, son. We will need dozens of these."

In a few minutes Papá lifted the cannoli out of the oil and slipped the crisp golden cones off the bamboo. As soon as they were cool enough, he, or others busy in the kitchen, would fill these cannoli shells with whipped ricotta cheese seasoned with sugar and citrus. Next they would be rolled in powdered sugar and placed on a tray ready to serve.

Besides Cannoli, there would be spumonti, an ice cream spliced with cake. The kitchen was full of other fancy pastas. Some sculptured pastries they had ordered from the Pasterio. And best of all came the molded ice cream called gelato.

The kitchen buzzed with merriment. *"Molta felecita!"* Nino liked to arrange the refreshments artistically on the buffet tables in the dining room. And he was present when the baby's *balia* (nurse) from a remote mountaintop village, had her first taste of ice cream. She found this nut-sprinkled texture so exquisite, it was unreal.

"Just wait," she told herself. "When my husband gets here, though maybe not today, he will have something so good he can't believe it!"

Nobody, however, noticed when she carefully lifted two ice creams off the tray and disappeared to her bedroom. She opened her trunk and placed the two gelati inside. Closing the lid, she thought, her eyes dancing, "These I have saved for my husband!"

Her *marido* finally did come, but not until the day after the fiesta. He had walked miles down steep mountain paths too narrow and rough, in places, for a donkey to go. His home was the very highest village in Sicily, and so primitive that people made their own shoes by sewing leather squares over their feet like an envelope. They used no currency for trade, only bartering with wine, oil or vegetables.

At the Rossi home at last, his wife greeted him with inklings of a great treat.

"Just wait, my husband," she promised, "I am bringing you something so delicious you cannot imagine it!"

She rushed to her trunk and opened the lid. No gelati! The paper was damp that had wrapped them. But the ice creams were gone, vanished. Her heart thumped with dismay. Immediately she cried for her signora, "Signorina, Signorina! Someone has played a trick on me and robbed my trunk."

"Why?" Signora Sara looked puzzled. "What makes you think so?"

"They aren't there! The gelati! I saved them to give to my husband! They are gone. Somebody must have taken them away!"

To the nurse's bewilderment, Signora simply shook her head. "No, Donna," she spoke gently, "gelato always melts unless kept on ice. But wait, let's see, maybe one is left." She stepped to the icebox and looked. "Yes. Here is another gelato. Take this to your husband."

He was as astounded as his wife knew he would be. *"Uttimo gusto!"* And the Talamo-Rossis could never forget the day the *balia* learned the secret mystique of ice cream.

To America

THAT DAY WAS BLACK as though the sun could never shine again. Church bells tolled her passing. In the Cathedral, novena candles flickered in the shadows. How could people even laugh again or children play? Anthony, fifteen, grieved deeply for his mother. At only thirty-nine she had died after a year's fight with cancer.

"If I only could have died instead of my mother." Nino could not bear to even go outside the house to see his friends. For a month he mourned, feeling his loss to the very depth of his being. "I remember how often mother said of those last months of her life. 'I hate to leave. I have a thorn in my heart. What will become of my two baby girls and my rascal boy, Nino?' " Nino could see her beautiful face, her perfect patrician features, her dark eyes full of kindness, her long hair worn in a simple bun. Whenever he had been naughty, her gentleness had melted him and more deeply moved him to be good than had his Papá's spankings. It seemed unbelievable that she was gone. December 1915 was only fourteen months from the glad day that Teresa was born. How thrilled she had been to have two daughters. Now Nino remembered the party of Teresa's baptism day, and how the house rang with the charm of Italian affection and merriment. He could hear them now, laughing together, when the nurse's husband saw Nino's father talking on the telephone on the wall. He had rushed to alarm his wife. "Look, look, our Signor is crazy. I saw him standing in the hallway and talking to the wall!" Soon corrected, he laughed jovially with others who also still marveled at the telephone and other wonders of the early twentieth century.

But in this time of deep grief, the boy Anthony matured rapidly, making that transition from childhood to becoming a man.

Not long after his mother's death, Adolfo's great uncle, Constantino Talamo-Rossi came to their home. He came from America. This fascinated young Anthony. The uncle had suffered a stroke and was paralyzed on one side. He hoped for recovery here in the sunshine and quiet lifestyle of Sicily at his great nephew's comfortable home near the hospital. Drawn to him like a magnet, Anthony waited on him day and night. He tried to anticipate his uncle's every want. Together by the hour, they talked of that magic place called America.

"Was Buffalo Bill real? Is America like Sicily?"

"No, not a bit like Sicily or Italy. Here workmen can earn

ten cents a day. Over there most anyone can earn a whole dollar a day."

"And New York? Can anybody find a job there, a place to live?"

As his invalid uncle answered questions and told stories of his own fabulous career—shipping sulphur to Europe, establishing railway systems, using five languages, one of them Russian, to aid United States diplomacy—Anthony built on all these facts the indestructable dream of going to America himself. "I will go to America," he vowed, "even if I have to swim the Atlantic."

Meanwhile, Anthony took his very first job and felt himself grown-up at last. He wore the cap of a trolley conductor, and every day he was assigned a trolley route in Messina and its environs. Often he got the route along the coast from Faro to Grampilier. The nice thing about this was that his petite Aunt Elvira, a wealthy lady, habitually prepared dinner for him when the trolley's last stop waited one half-hour at Grampilier. He loved seeing Zia Elvira and would always remember her hospitality. She owned a large property with many chestnut trees. Her cooking skill was irresistible! Others of the family Rossi liked to visit Zia, and she loved to have the little girls visit periodically for two weeks at a time.

But Anthony had to face the crisis every young man in Europe had to face at his age. He was seventeen and one-half now. Not only was military service mandatory for youth; but at this time Europe was still involved widely in World War One. Anthony would have to leave home for the army. The last day came for his trolley-car job and he would make it unforgettable to all who took the car from Faro to Grampilier. He sped the downhill tracks at a screaming pitch. His passengers, too aghast to utter a word, held on for dear life while Nino made his last run memorable. Ahead of time, yes, but provoking a squadron of angels to preserve his own tomorrows and those of others. It was a unique goodbye to his first and only job in Messina.

Italy had joined the Allies in the struggle for Europe. And the United States of America had entered the conflict, pouring forces into the lines of conflict. Anthony became a soldier in the Italian infantry. For a while his assignment was to be a Grenadier guard at the government palace. Tall, slender, fine looking—he was perfect for this honorable position.

Anthony's service in the military had extended beyond the armistice of November 11, 1918. Three years passed before he could return home, although he never had to see active service at the front. But, while he was in the army, Uncle Constantino died, and also his beloved grandmother Annetta.

Returning home from the army, Anthony noticed the many changes. Papá had a new wife whom the children called Zia Tina. Constantino and Alfredo were away at university. Joe was also gone and on his own now. The little girls were four and six, and young Salvatore had his turn receiving spankings. But such "persecution" at the hand of Zia Tina, Nino would not permit. He promptly disciplined her and raced away. Later, facing a Papá whose chagrin had faded, he, as usual, became the central interest of the family circle. They knew, however, that he hated to even unpack his suitcase. They saw that he was now determined to go to America.

Ships were booked. He had no money, no worldly goods, but also, no fears. The word "impossible" was not in his vocabulary. To his joy he would only have to wait ten days.

One morning, Carlo, who now worked for the White Star Shipping Lines, announced a vacancy. "One passenger, booked to leave tomorrow for America, is ill and cannot go."

"I will go!" Nino announced. Taking his obliging Papá, the two hurried from office to bank to office to acquire passport, borrow funds, purchase tickets in the one day before the ship was to sail. That evening, with his two suitcases in his hands, and thirty American dollars in his pocket Anthony told his family goodbye and took a train to Naples.

In the morning, he was up the gangplank and on the crowded liner. His heart skipped at the blast of the whistle. The ship slowly pushed away from its Italian port and gradually turned to the open sea.

This was not a luxury boat. In fact, passengers bunked in hammocks stretched across the decks. But the throb of the engines, the roll of the sea, the infinite indigo surface, the vast blue above—these things poured into the undaunted optimism of the Italian youth. His very soul was set on that wonderful new land, America.

At night, as Anthony lay awake in his hammock, he studied the light-pierced canopy above him. Those stars. "I love astronomy," he mused. And marveled that he could recognize several constellations. "I remember studying astronomy in the hospital in Rome while I was in the army." That had been a close call in his life.

One morning in his shower at the infantry barracks, he had stepped on a rusty nail. Neglecting to take notice of the injury, it became very sore, and when he noticed swelling and red streaks up his legs, he reported to the medical office. One glance showed the army doctor that Anthony already had blood poisoning. Promptly put in the hospital, nurses and doctors worked hard to pull him through. Gradually the high fever had subsided, and he felt the coolness and relief of the treatment reaching his bloodstream. However, convalescence was to be at least a month in the hospital. What to do? His busy mind hungered to learn, to feed upon something exciting. Then he asked, "Astronomy. I would love to learn about the stars. Could I please have an astronomy book to study?" The request granted, Anthony, always a good patient, was even better. His mind was challenged by the marvels of the universe beyond us. "How wonderful is God," he thought.

The voyage from Naples to New York was long. By the time it ended, Anthony had organized his knowledge of the city, knowledge gleaned from Uncle Constantino and others recently back from the United States.

"There she is!" He was thrilled. The Statue of Liberty was there where he expected her to be! Nor were the procedures at Ellis Island a surprise. He knew about taking the ferry to the Battery. He noted the location of the "Elevated" and already knew that a nickel would get him through the gate and onto the train. Confidence, not fear, marked him. He could tackle anything and be the winner.

Anthony was, at this time, devoutly Catholic. Yet his substantive knowledge of his faith was very small. He carried an image of the Madonna in his pocket for God's blessing, as Zia la Monica had told him. And when his feet first stood on American soil, a frantic prayer surged into his conscious thought. "God make me die if I fall in love with a Protestant girl. I don't want to go to hell!"

Knowing no English except "please," "yes," "no," and "I am hungry," Anthony spoke to the conductor on the Elevated: "Please, Bleeker Street."

"Yes," answered the courteous conductor. "I will tell you

the stop." Anthony knew he was on the 6th Avenue train. He knew he must get off at Bleeker Street. Near there he must look for an address on Thompson Street.

Alone—without language, known friend or money—yet Anthony was enthusiastic. He could imagine no obstacle, no danger that could possibly dismay him.

The train clicked past the numbers he expected to see. Up to a certain point all was well. Then the train rounded a long curve. Signs began to confuse Anthony. His memory list didn't match. He stepped up to the conductor again.

"Sir, please, Bleeker Street?"

With some consternation, the trainman indicated that they had passed Bleeker Street. "Get off at the next stop. Go back. Two stops back."

Anthony got off at the next stop and looked around to see where he could catch the train going the opposite direction. An Italian shoeshine boy was there to help. A melodic torrent of pure Italian was clear as day!

Boarding the train back, Anthony found the Bleeker Street stop with no trouble. Grasping two suitcases, his shoulders up, the slender young man walked briskly away from the traffic noise. He stopped and looked around to get his bearings. There in front of him was the sign, "Thompson Street." "Number 29," he read from his directions. Turning into the street he shortly found the house. Unbelievable! It read, "29 Thompson Street."

He was soon swept into a circle of friendly Italians. Yes! They knew of the prefect! Of course, their nephew was a male nurse in the hospital. And, true, there is a job for Anthony at an uncle's machine shop not far away.

"We will send someone along with you to make arrangements." And sure enough, the mechanic needed a helper to go with him to his job, to hand him tools and to learn the skills of installing zinc counters for changing restaurants into cafeterias.

"Tomorrow morning at seven o'clock we'll see you, young man. *Arrivederci!*"

And lodging? "Well, Anthony, there is an Italian family in West Broadway. They have a sixth-floor apartment and room for you to board there."

"Only a few hours here in this land. Yet I have a job and a place to stay already. I know it! America is the greatest, the most magnanimous country in the world!" Anthony had indeed discovered America, to love dearly and to belong to with pride.

Chicken Soup

ABRISK WIND RATTLED the frosty windows of the bedroom. At 5 o'clock A.M. the dollar alarm clock began to clang, sharply ending the cozy comfort of sleep. Nino opened his eyes and looked at the winder on the clock, spinning around as its whirring bells challenged. "Another day and to the machine shop by seven!" Anthony had worked overtime as usual the day before. Night slipped by abruptly.

Dressing quickly in the cold clapboard-walled room, Nino began to think through the day. "If only I could have a pot of chicken soup all cooked and ready when I come home tonight!" Now he was alone in the sparsely furnished apartment. The Italian family who had taken him as a boarder when he first came to America had returned to Italy for a visit.

Nino built a fire in the coal-burning stove in the kitchen. He then put a quarter in the slot for the two-burner gas stove so that he could make breakfast. The usual chores of getting off to work were almost mechanical. His mind was busy plotting a novel plan.

"I will find a way to cook that soup while I am away at work!"

The alarm clock with its twisting winder—there was the key. Thought and action coincided. He took the alarm clock over to the gas stove and tied its two legs firmly to the left burner on the stove. He then tied a cord to the winder of the clock. He also found a three-inch stick and bound it to the handle of the right burner on the stove, to lengthen it for better leverage. Taking the other end of the cord, he fastened it to the lengthened stove handle. The tension was just right.

"I've got it!" he said aloud to himself. Lighting the gas and turning the handle on, he then set off the alarm to test his scheme. Sure enough, the clock spun the cord around the winder so that the handle slowly but surely was pulled back into the off position, the gas flames disappeared.

"Now I will fix the soup!" Nino told the nobody there to listen. A pot of water, salt, a hen (bought yesterday at the market), an onion, a tomato, some celery and a large hunk of muscle bone. "Now it will need to cook for at least three hours."

He glanced at the time. It was about 6:30. Nino turned on the gas under the soup. He set the alarm clock at ten o'clock. The soup would cook slowly for three and a half hours.

"It will work!" Nino laughed. "Now I will only have to heat the soup when I come home tonight."

He left the apartment and skipped down six flights of steps to the predawn cold of New York City in winter. Anthony was off to his job with even more zest than usual. By working overtime, he was now earning the substantial sum of $35.00 per week.

A vigorous day's work ended at dusk. Nino raced up the six stairways and unlocked the door to his empty apartment. Inside was the warm aroma of chicken soup! Lifting the lid of the pot, he looked in. Perfect! The Big Ben clock anchored to the opposite burner had functioned precisely as planned. Tonight a favorite supper already waited hot and inviting. Like the renewed glow of the coal stove, the soup comforted the bleak apartment, transformed it into home. Anthony talked cheerfully to the clock and the stove, commending them, and sat down to enjoy his chicken soup. To him, as mechanic's apprentice, each day was chock-full of learning. So much to learn of: the job, the English language, New York and America! No wonder his joy bubbled over. Upbeat, eager and in love with thinking, inventing an automatic cooking device was just the greatest fun.

All around the Town

NEW YORK CITY ON A rainy day was bleak enough, but not to the driver of his very own shiny taxicab. Anthony drew up to a favorite pastry shop, bought an apple pie hot from the oven and promptly ate all of it with great relish. He was very young and very hungry. He could afford such luxury because a taxi driver could make twenty-five dollars on a day like this.

With a detailed map of the city, Nino was finding taxicabbing a great adventure. Only six months after he first came to the United States, he had been able to buy his first car, a used Buick. In another six months of learning his way around New York, he felt he could leave the machine shop for the cab business. He bought a Renault. It was great being on his own. Nobody could say the hours were too long. And money he earned added up enough to send some home to his father in Sicily, since there the family was large, and expenses, many.

Every time the check from America came, Signor Adolfo Talamo-Rossi would gather his sons and two little girls together and say to them, "See here, see what Nino is doing? See how he thinks about us." His tears of gratitude were sincere.

In New York an exuberant young man was glorying in his work—the greatest thing in life—a work to love and keep on learning in. He was also thinking ahead of new jobs to try, new business to create.

"Taxi driving is great. But with another kind of car, a cabriolet, I could become a chauffeur. That might be even better."

Chauffeur

MR. ROOT, NEPHEW OF the famous lawyer, Elihu Root, stood in front of his rather grand house. With his white gloves, he stiffly acknowledged the young man, Anthony Rossi, who had come to interview him for the position of chauffeur. Mr. Root drew back as Anthony walked closer to him. Feeling acutely insulted, Anthony, right then, decided to be hard-boiled. He did not care whether he got the position or not.

The brand-new-looking twin-six Packard Cabriolet, like a faithful steed, was parked close enough for scrutiny. Anthony was proud of it. Though he had paid only $250 for the car, he had painted and polished it to look elegant enough even for Mr. Root, chairman of the Hudson Manhattan Railroad.

"How much do you charge per month for your car and your services?" Mr. Root's correct speech was perfunctory, cold.

Anthony faced him with equal indifference. "$450 a month, sir."

"Well, uh, rather much, don't you think?" Mr. Root added, "But I suppose you paid quite a sum for that Cabriolet."

No response. Mr. Root began again. "$450 is a lot of money, I tell you. Think it over and telephone me if you change your mind."

"Yes," Anthony answered sternly.

Mr. Root sensed a tone of finality and continued, "I will phone you if I decide it is a deal."

Anthony pulled away with a feeling of relief. Mr. Root was known to be eccentric. He would not read a newspaper without wearing gloves. People, as well, were untouchable.

However, as soon as Anthony reached his apartment, the phone was ringing. Mr. Root had decided. "Meet me at my home at 1:15 P.M. sharp. You will take me to my office at Cortland and Church Streets, and come for me at 4 o'clock to bring me back home."

In the Cabriolet, the chauffeur sat in a separate compartment open on the sides. The back seat was entirely enclosed. Mr. Root directed his chauffeur by a system he had contrived.

"If we are stopped, I ring the bell once to go. If we are going, I ring the bell once to stop. To turn right, I ring the bell twice; to turn left, three times." In this way, no conversation between chauffeur and passenger was ever necessary.

Besides the five-day trips to the office, Anthony would

take Mr. Root on weekends for a drive around Central Park and along Riverside Drive. Also, during the fall and winter season, he would chauffeur Mr. Root to pick up Miss Vanderbilt and take her to the opera every Friday evening. At 7:55 P.M. the Cabriolet would stop within one block of the Vanderbilt house on 5th Avenue and 52nd Street. At exactly one minute to eight, the bell would ring and the Cabriolet would then move slowly forward to reach the house punctually at eight o'clock.

Anthony did find that $450 a month was a large amount for so light a routine. He had plenty of spare time for taxicabbing in the mornings and many more projects besides— all steppingstones to bigger things to come. New ideas were brewing.

Of Eggs and Cheese

O N THE TOP RUNG of the stepladder, Anthony dipped his brush into a bucket of white paint. The smallish room must have clean white walls and ceiling. Every wall must be lined with shelves for canned goods and staples. Display racks on the floor to the right would be filled with tea, coffee, and special fancy canned goods. In the back center an ice box was already installed to keep an ample supply of fresh eggs.

In fact, this grocery had evolved out of a spare-time sideline of collecting eggs from the country and selling them door to door. Brother Joe, now in New York, took part in the venture. Anthony had bought a second-hand Lincoln and removed the back seat so that it could be used as a truck.

After the second or third day of selling eggs, some disturbing complaints came in.

"Don't you candle the eggs?"

"Candle the eggs?" Nino was bewildered. "What do you mean, 'Candle the eggs'?" Neighbors then explained that in order to discard eggs with traces of blood in them, candling must be done. Each egg must be examined through a gadget with light which could detect any dark indication of blood. Even in the simple task of selling eggs, there was much to learn!

Anthony found, however, that he could sell the discarded eggs for a bargain price to bakeries. And the neighborhood egg vending grew so popular that grocery stores asked for supplies of the country fresh eggs.

Inevitably, the grocery business intrigued Anthony, teasing him to enter a new world of knowledge and business expertise. He sold his chauffeuring car and job to a friend; his two taxi cabs as well.

He found a place in an ideal location and bought it. An attractive grocery store emerged called Aurora Farms—"Our specialty—eggs only one day old."

The corner grocery in Jackson Heights, Long Island, would become immediately popular for its choice inventory of quality brands and reasonable prices plus its enthusiastic service.

Nino was doing a neat job of the painting. He hoped to open the store in only two more days.

"Hey, Sir, good morning!" Nino turned from his painting and looked down into the ruddy face of the cheese salesman.

"You will want cheese in your store, sir. I sell fine

cheeses. When do you want some?"

"Why, yes. Cheese. We open day after tomorrow."

"What cheeses do you want, sir?"

Nino thought, "What do I know about cheese?" But he replied, "Friend, you know the kinds of cheese people like around here. Bring me a selection of the popular brands."

"When do you want them, sir?"

"Come back in two days and, please, as you see I am so busy, be sure to bring with you a list of the cheeses showing for each one the wholesale and retail prices. Can I depend on you for this?"

"Yes, sir. I will be back in two days."

"Friday he will be back," thought Anthony. "I must install a cheese display counter and have it ready." Working night and day, Nino did manage to get the store in shape for the opening day.

Early Friday, the cheese man appeared with an array of items.

"Good morning, sir. I have the cheese. Shall I leave it here?"

"Say, listen, you see how busy we are. Would you please arrange the cheese on this showcase so that the name of each kind can be seen clearly? Also, if you hand me the list of prices, I want to stick it up behind the cheese counter for my convenience."

The cheese salesman did a neat job of displaying his cheeses and left. Moments later, a customer arrived. "Lellecranz cheese. Do you have any?"

"Lellecranz, did you say?" he asked, having never heard of it himself. "Can you see? I can't see it from here! Will you just have a look and see if you can find it?"

"Oh, yes. Here it is. How much, sir?"

Messina, Sicily, Anthony Rossi's birthplace, as it looks today.

Anthony Rossi (center) with his staff in one of New York's first large supermarkets which he owned in the 1930s.

Tropic Ana became the logo for Tropicana in 1950, and still appears on the company's products today.

In the late 1940s and 1950s Tropicana's fleet of refrigerated trucks, operating out of Bradenton, Florida, grew steadily.

In February 1957 the S.S. Tropicana, the world's first sea-going ship devoted to transporting fresh-squeezed orange juice by volume, made its maiden voyage from Port Canaveral, Florida, to Long Island pier at Whitestone in New York. The ship carried 1,450,000 gallons of juice.

Anthony Rossi and Ed H. Price, Jr., executive vice president of Tropicana, inspect the Tropicana train which initiated service on June 1, 1970.

The mile-long Tropicana train consisted of 150 refrigerated railroad cars especially designed and constructed for Tropicana. It was able to make the trip from Florida to New York in 36 hours.

BEVERAGE WORLD

May 1977

It's not just for breakfast anymore°

Anthony T. Rossi, founder, president
and chairman of the board Tropicana Products, Inc.

How to sell to the fast food market

The billion dollar drink mix boom

Anthony Rossi and Tropicana were featured on the May 1977 cover of Beverage World *magazine.*

Among his many awards and honors, Anthony Rossi received an honorary doctorate in humane letters from the University of Tampa on April 26, 1980.

The Tropicana plant in Bradenton, Florida, employs over 2,800 people.

Rossi's interest in Christian missions brought him to Columbia Bible College in Columbia, South Carolina.

In the 1960s and 1970s the Rossi's visited Sicily each year. They helped establish a church in Anthony Rossi's hometown of Messina through home Bible studies, public lectures and open-air preaching, as seen above in this 1970 photograph.

The Bradenton Missionary Village, begun in 1981, accommodates 235 retired missionary families.

Quickly Nino checked the list behind the counter. Lelle-cranz cheese—33 cents wholesale, 36 cents retail. "It is 36 cents a pound, madam."

Grocery business was great. Nino had the knack of remembering details and never forgetting. He soon knew the price of all his inventory and never failed to recall each one accurately.

Aurora Farms was a busy and favorite store in Jackson Heights, Long Island.

Aurora Farms Again

THE CORNER GROCERY in Jackson Heights flourished. Business was thriving even in the depression.

Then one day a man offered Nino about $30,000 for the store and all its inventory. Impulsively he sold it and decided to try out the restaurant business. His zest for new ventures and new knowledge carried Anthony forward to bigger and bigger enterprises. But in a year or so, he noticed one day that the corner grocery was empty.

"What happened?" he inquired.

"Well, they gave it up. It didn't do well, so they left." Anthony felt keen nostalgia for his Aurora Farms grocery. So much so that he left the restaurant to brother Joe, bought back the corner store and opened for business.

As before, the place became very popular. Jackson Heights neighbors were delighted that Tony Rossi was back.

Among those who came to work in the store was a boy fifteen years old. He came bouncing in early one morning.

"Could you use an errand boy, sir?" he addressed Anthony earnestly.

"Your name is?"

"Santo, Santo Consiglio."

"Well, Santo, we could use you. I believe you will be a good errand boy."

Quickly Santo responded, "How much do you pay, sir?"

"Fifteen dollars a week."

"Great, I'll take the job!"

"Here, Santo, is your first order to deliver. With it is the address in Jackson Heights." So bent on getting on with the job, Santo grabbed the bundle of groceries and tore for the door with such momentum that he bumped into a customer coming in. An astounded lady, picking herself up, heard only. "Whoops, excuse me please!"

Something else added new excitement to Aurora Farms grocery. A certain young lady in the neighborhood would come in and select her favorite things. When she entered, the whole place seemed under a spell. Nino had never met anyone like Miss Florence Stark. Her manner was cultured, gentle, kind. "Miss Stark is very special," Nino thought to himself. This was a novel thing for him who was all work and not easily influenced by feminine charms.

"May I leave these groceries here?" Florence was asking. Her eyes were always alight, ready to laugh, full of latent humor. "Until I come back from the butcher shop?"

"Why certainly." Nino, glad to do a favor, practically insisted that she leave them. He would take care of them.

While Florence Stark was away, Anthony got busy. He hunted and found several large jars of Smucker's jellies. These he put in the bottom of the carton containing Florence's groceries.

"Now, she won't be able to lift this!" he plotted. Sure enough, when Florence returned to pick up her groceries, she was startled to find them so heavy.

"Why," she said, "I didn't know I bought so much."

"Never mind, Miss Stark," hoping he looked casual, "I will have them sent to your apartment."

"Well, thank you very much. I do appreciate this service. Goodbye."

Later, who should be errand boy but Anthony himself! He carried the groceries to Florence Stark's apartment.

This began a significant friendship, and in awhile, a long engagement, and eventual marriage. Florence Stark was the daughter of a Methodist minister, now deceased. She held a very responsible position as the secretary to Dr. Acheson, prominent inventor, scientist and good friend of Thomas Edison. However, she had promised him never to marry as long as she was his secretary. And this promise she kept until he died.

Meanwhile, Anthony sold the Aurora grocery again. This time in order to move down the street to a larger place where he became one of the first in New York City to start a self-service market.

At this time he also marketed fresh fruits and vegetables. This meant getting up before daybreak to make it to the open markets to select choice produce at bargain prices. By doing this, he kept his own produce fresh and choice— another reason his store was popular and successful.

By this time Nino's age (with the century) was in the late thirties. Married to Florence at last, he dreamed onward toward greater ventures.

"New York is too cold, Florence. Have you ever been to Florida?"

A Wonderful Discovery

IF WE GO SOUTH, Florence, I think I will do farming. I like farming."

"What kind of farming?"

"I don't know exactly. I think I will go to the library and find out about agriculture in the South, particularly in Florida." Anthony had already sold the market in order to have the free time he needed as they prepared to leave New York and move south. At the Library on 42nd Street and 5th Avenue, a librarian helped locate a current book on agriculture. It had chapters on tomato growing in the southern States. Taking the book to one of the long library tables, Anthony sat down to study. But right there on the table he saw a book. Someone had failed to return it to the shelf. The title caught his attention: *The Life of Christ.*

"Why, I don't know anything about Christ except that he was a baby in the Madonna's arms and that he died on the cross." He opened the book and began to read. Transfixed, he forgot about farming. The story of Christ began to unfold. Hours passed.

He took a break for lunch to run over to Horn and Hardet to coin-grab a sandwich and coffee and hurry back to read more.

"This is wonderful!" He closed the book late one afternoon. "But why don't I go now to the source? Tomorrow I am going to get the Bible itself."

So engrossed in reading the Bible, Anthony let the days flow by. Every day he poured over the pages of a book so new to him, so filled with answers. Beginning with Genesis, he read of creation and of the beginnings of God's converse with mankind. The history, fascinating in itself, made God so real, His character so clear, right and wrong so definite and absolute. Coming to the Psalms, he felt impatient to pick up the narrative again. He skipped sections in haste to get to the New Testament. From morning until night, he read the book. Much he did not understand, but now he was captured in the realization that this was something real and very important that he had never known or discovered before. In the last book of the Old Testament he noticed the passage, "But unto you that fear my name shall the Sun of righteousness arise with healing in His wings" (Mal 4:2 KJV).

Then came Matthew, the first book in the New Testament. He was profoundly impressed by the Sermon on the Mount. The lessons taught to the disciples, the miracles, the crucifixion account. But, oh, the Resurrection of Jesus Christ. How strategic! He proceeded to Mark's swift account corroborating Matthew. Then to Luke and the beautiful story of the shepherds at Bethlehem.

When he reached the fourth Gospel, Anthony pondered over the simple words of John 3:16: "For God so loved the world, that He gave His only begotten Son, that whosoever believeth in Him should not perish, but have everlasting life" (KJV). The message was so clear, sincere, consistent throughout the Bible.

"Why do I need to fear purgatory? Why do I need to do penance for sins, pray for the dead whom I have loved? Christ has already died to pay for all my sins and to forgive each person who trusts Him."

Every chapter held so much that even he could grasp and find enlightening. He read on so glad for every truth he could comprehend and appreciate.

After reading the Bible in the New York City library, Anthony's personal faith found footing on a new plateau. God was near, real, predictable. He joined the First Methodist Church with Florence when they came to Florida in 1941. And yes, Anthony Rossi planted tomatoes on a 50-acre lease near Cortez Road in Bradenton. Perhaps his fixed career would be farming. Maybe?

Farming

THE ROSSIS HAD FIRST spent one year in Cape Charles, Virginia, farming tomatoes. Then they decided to move on to Florida. Bradenton, at that time a small and rural town on the central west coast, was a great place for growing tomatoes. It became their choice.

Anthony's fifty acres on Cortez Road kept him intensely busy—preparing the soil, beginning the tomato plants from seeds, and then transplanting them row after row while directing and supervising the hired helpers.

"Tony, you can't pay men a dollar a day. It's hard on the rest of us. We pay 75¢." This comment received no reply. Farming was demanding work. Cultivating required labor from January until April when the first crop ripened. But how satisfying to see the field produce a record crop!

When Anthony first began this task, he talked about it with God who was so much a part of his thinking since he had discovered the Bible.

"Father," he prayed unpretentiously, "if I make $5,000 net profit on these tomatoes, I will be satisfied." Wasn't it alright to talk to God about everything? At first, it looked as though the tomatoes would bring in far more profit than that. But when the hour came to harvest them, troubles developed.

"Not enough pickers, Florence! We're going to lose lots." All available pickers had been hired earlier by experienced tomato farmers all around him.

"Impossible to find the pickers we need." Anthony also found he could not get enough boxes for the marketing of his tomatoes. Lacking experience in tomato farming was partly the cause of this twofold emergency. Despite his practical ingenuity and hard work, Anthony had to watch a large portion of perfect tomatoes rot on the ground. He simply could not get them to the market.

Florence carefully tallied the books and came up with news. "Nino, we have made a net profit of exactly $5,000."

"God did just what I asked, Florence." It was awesome to realize the reality of communion with the Lord who lives and is near. Anthony was grateful. Yet, to tell the truth, he also remarked about this phenomenon, "Shucks, I should have asked God for $10,000!"

God's reality stayed in the headlines of his thoughts. "He does hear me. He is real—the living God."

The Floridian

FARMING OR BUSINESS? Which should I do? I like both."
Anthony pondered these questions for days. He prayed to
understand God's direction in his life.

One morning while downtown a friend hailed him and
crossed the street to talk. "Say, Tony, did you know this
cafeteria is for sale?" The friend pointed to the Floridian
right on the corner of Sixth Avenue and Twelfth Street where
they stood.

"True?"

"I understand Mr. Burgess has another cafeteria in New
York. He wants to concentrate on that one and sell the
Floridian."

"That's interesting. Thanks for letting me know." And before the friend had crossed Sixth Avenue, Anthony Rossi was inside the cafeteria and looking for Mr. Stafford Burgess. He found him.

"Is it true this cafeteria is for sale?"

"Yes, it is." Mr. Burgess then told him he wanted $8,000 cash for the building and the business.

Here was the answer to Anthony's questioning—farming or business. His heart beat fast. This was exciting. God was leading him! Promptly Anthony consulted his lawyer, Mr. Dewey Dye, and they met together with Mr. Burgess. The transaction was completed. Anthony paid Burgess $8,000 cash, and the cafeteria, so suddenly, was his.

"Can you believe it, Florence. Just today I am the owner and manager of the Floridian Cafeteria!"

Without pause, the cafeteria continued as usual, even in the midst of renovations Anthony found necessary. The wall facing Sixth Avenue was chiseled out for large front windows to let in more light. The small ceiling fan he replaced with a very large more effective one. In spite of the redecorating activities, planned, of course, for off hours, the cafeteria continued service as usual. The cafeteria began to "make waves" in downtown Bradenton.

"Who would be a better chef than my own brother Joe?" Anthony reasoned. He telephoned Joe in Chicago where he was head chef in a large hotel. "Joe, I need you here in Bradenton, Florida. Can you come right away and take over the kitchen?" Within one week, Joe was the Floridian's chief chef. With great gusto, he worked with his brother.

Anthony selected and purchased all the food, providing quality brands of everything. Thomas breads and English muffins came from New York. Best cheeses, olive oil, vinegar, olives, et cetera, came imported from Italy.

"The food must be good, top in quality and taste!" The taster in the kitchen, Anthony himself, had to be pleased.

The Floridian became popular from the day Anthony took it over. People came all the way from Sarasota to enjoy Friday's specialty of meatballs and spaghetti. On Sunday at noon, the line of people filing into lunch was two blocks long.

Florence saw to it that a fresh rose was on each table every day. She also took care of the canary songster in its pedestal cage and served as bookkeeper and accountant. In the cafeteria's first year, its net profit was $35,000.

Each Sunday morning, Anthony provided a devotional time, having pastors alternately to preside. People had urged him to offer beer among the beverages, but he refused to have any alcoholic drinks in his cafeteria. God had led him to this business. He would try to honor God in it.

But success to Anthony was not to be a status quo to rest on. Rather, it became fresh incentive to press forward, to expand. Making money had already become a means of being more useful to others. He now dreamed of a second cafeteria, perhaps a chain of them in the future. Could it be in Lakeland, Tampa, Orlando, or even Miami? The dynamics of business, he knew innately, should never become static. He would push to bigger ventures.

The Terrace Restaurant

FLORENCE, I HAVE FOUND it! Just the place for us. It is the largest restaurant south of Washington D.C. and right on Miami Beach!"

"A restaurant, Nino, and not a cafeteria?"

"Well, it also has a coffee shop on one side. You watch though. It will be the greatest restaurant around!"

"How much is it?"

"It rents for $14,500 a year. We'll have a ten-year lease." Anthony and Florence then moved to Miami. Hard work, long hours never deterred Anthony. He saw to it that the spacious restaurant had new red plush carpeting, a parquet-floored dancing area which he helped to build. It would also be the stage for a twelve-piece orchestra.

"We'll have concert music and a singer in the evenings."

This beautiful place had the capacity to seat 500 guests at a time. And the coffee shop also was already doing a thriving business.

With no time lost, The Terrace was opening its doors to Miami's residents and tourists. Directly across the street from the Runi Plaza Hotel, the restaurant held a promising location. The Rossis were sure it would be a success.

Nevertheless, July 1944 was not an auspicious time. World War two was at a critical stage. The Nazis had broken the French lines. For the Allies, winning the war was still not assured. Gas rationing restricted tourists. Even at Miami Beach they were few, and traffic was minimal. Everywhere business suffered as overseas causes grew. Yet none of these dark clouds on the horizon darkened Anthony's optimism. The Terrace would offer the very finest in menus and entertainment.

But, as weeks went by, Anthony never saw the dining areas completely full. Where were the hundreds it welcomed and prepared to serve?

Day after day, hopes rose in the morning, to drop out of sight by midnight. The people were just not there.

Nino woke up to the sickening fact that he was losing $1,000 a day. He worked harder, trying new ways to interest larger numbers to come. Yet the daily loss was a consistent $1,000.

Deep in his soul Nino felt he knew why this was happening. He had, early on, yielded to the insistent urging to sell alcoholic beverages. "I won't sell liquor," he had first remonstrated when well-meaning friends told him that people would not come to the restaurant otherwise.

"But Tony," they pleaded, "you can get no business at all if you don"t sell drinks. Nobody around here will come."

Succumbing at last to the pressure and the logic, Nino had conceded.

"I will sell liquor, O.K. But only at the table. I will not have a bar."

Now as The Terrace stayed in the red daily, Anthony knew in his heart that he himself was the Jonah. He was the guilty one. And God could not bless him. In two or three months, he had lost all his savings. To shore up the failing restaurant, he decided he must sell the Floridian in Bradenton; Mr. Caruso of Lionel Trains was happy to buy it from him for $35,000 cash.

In one month, all of this money was gone. Anthony felt deeply chastised and repentant. At the foot of his bed, he knelt and cried with tears, beseeching God for forgiveness. "I am sorry. I deserve this spanking," he said.

On December 28, 1944, five months into The Terrace Restaurant business, the situation had become acute. With only $3,000 in the bank, Anthony had to pay the debt of $18,000 by the first of January. This was money to be paid for salaries and liquor license. He did not know where to turn.

That day in the afternoon, Mr. E. M. Loews (of Loews Theaters) came to the Terrace. "May I see you, Mr. Rossi?"

"Certainly," Anthony responded. "Come into my office and we will talk."

Mr. Loews had an exciting idea: "What about having an international cuisine here? You need something different to attract people. One week you could serve Hungarian food, the next, French, then Italian, and so on. People may be drawn in by the novelty of the menus from other countries."

Anthony listened. It did seem like a great idea. "Perhaps—" But just then his phone rang.

Answering, Anthony heard a man introducing himself as a realtor. "Mr. Rossi, would you be interested in selling your restaurant?" "Well, it all depends . . . what are you talking about?" Mr. Loews, hearing it all, stage whispered to Anthony, "Go ahead. Don't be afraid. Go see what it is all about."

Feeling, then, that he would not be letting Mr. Loews down in any way, he consented to go immediately to the realty office. There he discovered that Mr. Lou Walters was anxious to buy a place on Miami Beach. He was stuck out in the suburbs where rationing nullified his night-club business.

"Tell him," Anthony stated, "That The Terrace sells for $65,000 cash, plus the cost of food and liquor."

The realtor had Walters on the phone immediately. "Get him to stay right there. I'll be at your office in thirty minutes."

Lou Walters could not agree to pay $65,000 cash, but he did settle for immediate payment of $20,000 and a monthly $10,000 until the total would be completed. With lawyers on hand, the deal was made. Lou Walters, father of television news reporter Barbara Walters, bought the restaurant. He did not want the food and liquor since he had his own. These were sold to other restaurants in the vicinity.

"Florence, I feel like bushel bags of potatoes have been taken off my shoulders! Just in time, God has helped us!"

Falling to his knees again in the quiet of his bedroom, Anthony thanked God for such a remarkable deliverance—just in time to pay off all debts! The burden of failing business was lifted and taken forever away. And this lesson

learned would never be forgotten: the principles of disobe-
dience, punishment, repentance and restoration.

Remembering this Miami experience, Anthony has often
declared, "I thank God for the spanking. By this, he turned
me back into the path of his direction in my life."

Tomorrow a vacuum? By no means. New ideas came with
the sunrise. The road ahead widened. Bigger, even glorious
years would run to meet him.

"I have found out," Anthony confided, "that God loves
me. And all God does is for my own good."

Gift Boxes of Florida Citrus

ANTHONY ROSSI STOOD at the produce counter in one of Miami's supermarkets. Taking plenty of time and care, he wanted to select the fruit himself—the largest oranges, the finest grapefruit. The job of preparing and shipping citrus fruit in fancy gift boxes, he had started the same week he sold The Terrace Restaurant two years ago. Others were also doing this. Anthony found he could compete in the marketplace in two ways. He could make sure his fruit boxes were superior in quality, and he could see that they sold for less than those of all competitors. Total dedication and his inbuilt creativeness tipped the scales in his favor. Like anything he did, his whole heart was in it—the most important thing in the world!

"Anthony," Florence told her husband, "remember my niece Dorothy Brown with her husband Robert, are living here in Miami now. I feel sure they will be interested in helping us in this gift box business!" And Dorothy and Bob joined in the effort, catching the same fervor and delight in the work.

"Can you believe it, Anthony!" Dorothy was laughing with their discovery. "A store space available on Flageller Street in wartime when space is practically unobtainable?"

"It is just right for us!" Anthony, who had found it first, agreed. In no time their store windows displayed sample gift boxes and their bargain prices. Dorothy kept busy daily at her desk, receiving customers and orders.

Not far away in a small packing house, the choice fruit was washed and artistically arranged in boxes according to the specified orders. Often these included candies as well.

Week by week, Anthony, in controlling the business, sought untiringly to improve time efficiency, labor relations and net profits. (Costs per box were at about $2.50 and the gift box sold for around $5.50.) Sales gained. Competition favored them. And Bob Brown began collecting orders from the shippers in other stores. Soon nearly everyone around wanted Rossi's gift fruit. Orders poured in. The demand was challenging, but their boxes continued selling cheaper and buyers got excellent service. Everything looked great!

But Anthony was not satisfied. "We do the wrong thing, Bob." Brown listened with surprise. "I could go back to Bradenton and buy the fruit from the trees much cheaper."

The logic precipitated the return of Anthony and Florence Rossi to Bradenton. They left the Browns in Miami to handle orders there.

In Bradenton, Anthony's first concern was to find a suitable packing house. Again, he was struck with God's providence. On the very day he began to search, he found the place exactly right for him. Located beside the railroad tracks, the two-hundred-foot-long warehouse was fully equipped with machinery for sizing, washing and polishing the citrus fruit. Its owner had died and it had remained unused for two years. Today it was selling for only $3,000. Again, impressed with God's provision, Anthony bought the plant without hesitation on the same day he found it.

Picking crews, working in three shifts, brought in oranges and grapefruit from the groves. They were thirty-five cents a box plus fifteen cents for picking and delivery. "Bob," Anthony fairly shouted over the phone, "we have reduced our cost per box from $2.50 to 50 cents! Now we can cut the sale price on the boxes to $3.50.

Next word from Bob Brown was that the sales of gift fruit had crescendoed. Anthony arranged to drive weekly to Naples, Florida, meeting Bob halfway so that detailed orders from Miami could be listed and discussed. From Bradenton (actually the warehouse was in Palmetto just across the the bordering Manatee River) two carloads of gift fruit boxes were shipped out each day via Railway Express for northern destinations. The business peaked.

But at this point a new dilemma arose, a consequence that would become a new steppingstone—in fact, this time, a giant one. The bulk fruit from the groves was carefully picked through to select the large fruit. These were choice for the gift boxes. Yet what about the abundant fruit left over?

"Those little oranges! What must I do with the small grapefruit and oranges?" Anthony thought carefully, pondering this matter. And a new enterprise emerged—an exciting first for Florida.

Fruit Industries, Inc.

STEEP BUILDINGS BLOCKED off the sky into wisps of cloud above the agitated traffic below. New York City was a far cry from the small quiet town of Bradenton, Florida, on Tampa Bay. Nevertheless, Anthony was in New York in search of Santo Consiglio. This intelligent, capable young friend of grocery store days years past could be a key to marketing citrus products in the big city.

At this time, Anthony was aware that the Waldorf-Astoria was buying citrus fruit in the markets and employing forty women in their downtown kitchen to cut up the fruit. They were also squeezing their own oranges for juice. This was considerably costly. But the fresh citrus sections and juice were popular salads and appetizers.

"Hotels like the Waldorf would love to have the oranges and grapefruit from Florida already prepared! And the fresh-squeezed juice! They will recognize the economy of this from their own viewpoint!" Anthony thought audibly. Hearing the words aloud he was convinced he was not stretching the truth.

"Impossible, Tony," his friends had told him. "The fruit will spoil in transit. You have to cook it and can it. The flavor, then, will be flat. I"m afraid the idea just can't work." Anthony listened silently to these very sound objections from those who understood the perishable food business. Nevertheless, "impossible" happened to be a word that was not in Anthony Rossi's vocabulary.

"If I can only find Santo," he mused. "He and I can work together. He will believe with me that this can be done." And he inquired among friends in New York. "Where is Santo Consiglio now?" And they responded.

"We hear he is back in New York from the war and that he lives in a low-rent apartment complex below Jackson Heights in Long Island City!"

Locating the huge apartment complex, Nino looked at the fifty or sixty large buildings behind the main entrance from the street. "How can I hope to discover Santo's place among all these?" Although a bit set back, Anthony knew God would guide him. He approached the first building. "Hundreds of people live in this one, I'm sure." But as he looked at the index of occupants posted near the door, he read aloud, "Santo Consiglio, apartment 205!" Incredible! The first name he focused on in the very first apartment building! Nino's heart sang. Sure enough the buzzer found Santo at home.

Nino then told Santo his strategy for the brand-new Fruit Industries, Inc., in Florida. They conversed in excitable English—the English that New Yorkers can claim exclusively. Glowing, they both emerged from those hours of creative discussion with a new chapter begun for each of them.

The next day, Santo freed himself from his job at Borden and joined Anthony. First they had to find a suitable office and refrigerated storage space to begin fresh citrus distribution. And sure enough, in the Atlas Terminal Buildings, they found the ideal place for them in the commercial zone.

"How will you get the fruit up here without spoilage, Tony?" Santo grinned. He knew Nino would have this solution. And he did.

"Santo, refrigerated trucks they have now are not cold enough. True, the fruit sections would spoil if we used them. But we will pack the gallons of fruit solids and orange juice into a trailer-truck. We will blow chipped ice into it so that it is packed solidly. Then we'll put a thick canvas over it. We will schedule regular stops along the way to blow fresh crushed ice over it for the one-and-a-half-day's trip to New York. I promise you, Santo, the citrus will be absolutely fresh when you receive it. That garage we have bought for our plant here has adequate drainage for dumping the ice from the truck. You can immediately store the glass jars of fruit and juice in the refrigerated room at this place. Of course, Santo, you will sell it right away!"

Within weeks the work in New York began. Santo addressed his task with typical ingenuity and verve, totally identified with the exciting new industry. Owning the very first truck labeled, "Fruit Industries," he loaded up with fruit sections and juice in jars, and hurried off to sell the Florida specialties in the great New York hotels.

But all did not go smoothly. Sometimes tie-ups in transport from Florida to New York caused spoilage. Precious gallons of produce had to be thrown away. But Santo persevered stubbornly. He and Anthony were a team, and for either to give up or become discouraged would be unforgivable.

Back in Bradenton, Anthony was setting up a new and larger plant on Manatee Avenue East. It was close to the railroad tracks and across the street from the Sea Board Station. Behind three rows of long stainless steel counters, fifty or more young women in white uniforms and rubber gloves took the whole fruit, already peeled, from the conveyor belt, and with sharp knives, swiftly and deftly cut up the fruit, making sure no seeds were left in each section. Anthony himself had carefully taught them this skill. The girls packed the jars artistically—a layer of grapefruit, a layer of oranges, a layer of pineapple. These were the jars labeled "Fruit Salad." Others were packed with grapefruit and oranges alone.

Beyond the rows of "sectionizers," hummed the extractor, juicing the small oranges to make pure, natural juice. Soon it was chilled and bound for New York's fancy hotels. Until shipped, the citrus jars kept cool and fresh in the refrigerated room next to the sectionizing area.

Telephone wires between Anthony and Santo tingled with new progress reports. "Everybody wants the fruit, Tony," Santo shouted. "I need more trucks, Tony."

First it was ten more trucks for Santo—then more and more. Dairy trucks from all over the city came to Santo's plant to load up, adding juice and sections to their assortment of milk and cheeses for daily delivery to customers. Soon more then a hundred trucks were delivering citrus products along with their milk and cream.

The phoneline from Santo constantly rang out the great news, "The fruit just arrived this afternoon, Tony. And it is fresh as a rose."

Growth became the essence of the new company: more fruit, more employees, more space, more transport. Fruit Industries, Inc., soon overtook the gift box business which was then discontinued. The new fruit sections and juice enterprise took first place, and later claimed Anthony's total attention.

"Fruit Industries," Nino thought aloud. "I don't like that name. It is too dull." Aware of God's help in every step, he prayed for a better name for the new company. And right at that moment as he was driving south on 41, The Tamiami Trail, an attractive motel sign caught his eye along the road somewhere south of Sarasota. It read, "Tropicana Cabins." Thrust into his mind was an immediate answer to his request.

"Tropicana! That's it. I like the name Tropicana. Our company shall be called Tropicana."

Early Tropicana

SUMMER EVENING AROUND nine o'clock held fast to the day. Some light and vivid red-gold sunset hallowed its ending. They had worked late again this Tuesday. Anthony and Florence, with their beautiful German Shepherd, Lady, came home and closed the front door. The phone was ringing. Anthony's long stride brought him instantly to answer it.

"Oh, Santo! How is everything?" Florence, hustling to get a light supper on the table, heard bits of the electric dialog. The fruit sections were much in demand in New York City. New improved refrigerated trucks came in loaded. Yet they were bringing barely enough to meet the market demand. Santo's imperative did not change. "Tony, we want *more*. We have a standing order for 1,000 gallons a week for the Waldorf-Astoria alone. Get more truckloads to us. Can you, Tony? Also the demand for the fresh juice is increasing. This goes out on the dairy delivery vans."

Tropicana was in full swing indeed. It was 1950. Florence often spoke to her husband about how happy she was with the new name for the company, Tropicana. To play on the word, the logo became Tropic Ana—the little girl in her tropic grass shirt, holding a basket of oranges on her black pigtailed head.[1] The pose for the model Anthony demonstrated, and five-year-old Chrissie Kesten became the perfect model.

"Jane Beckley can sketch and paint it for us," Florence commented. And she did, giving the logo a pixie touch. It became distinctly a winner.

Even though Tropicana was becoming central in their lives, Florence and Anthony, along with about two-dozen other friends, had the joy of seeing a new church begin in Bradenton. They started as a chapel of the First Methodist church in town, meeting, at first, in the Manatee High School. Florence and Anthony were the first names on the list of charter members. Among these were Murray and Peggy Kesten, Nettie and Jim Pratt, Vera and Jim Marley, Doug and Marge Bell, Harry and Martha Evelyn Parham, Ed and Elsie Price, with many other friends who filled that charter member roll. This was a spiritually hungry group, eager to learn more about the Bible and to experience God's working in their lives.

On the very first Sunday the church opened, a pipe organ appeared—a gift to the new church. No one told who had presented it. They remained anonymous. Yet the organ was installed just in time for the first service. Florence and her reliable housekeeper and cook, Mary Daughtry, had arranged flowers to decorate the sanctuary for its opening. The Rossis and their charter member friends found much joy in giving to the Lord's work. This they prepared to do frequently and established the Trinity Foundation to carry out this new goal. The dozen or so members of the new foundation would find it a tangible means of showing their love for God.

They, as young couples, were discovering that God could do wonders for them in their own personal lives. Some had been restored from alcoholism and various difficulties. In gratitude they felt compelled to help others, share in counseling them, relating their own testimonies.

But, at this stage in their Christian experience, their faith was the first light of dawn, not yet wholly spread with that sunrise to come later. Yet they were discovering that "Blessed are they which do hunger and thirst after righteousness: for they shall be filled" (Mt 5:6 KJV).

In the year of 1950, Mary Daughtry's first son Charles was born. Mary was very much a part of the Rossi household; a loyal and capable young black woman, she was more than maid. Mary was a trusted friend. Florence stood by Mary in her time of need and her difficult delivery. At last Charles the healthy baby arrived, and Mary soon bounced back to her normal energy and good health. Charles Daughtry was born April 16, 1950.

In April of 1951, when Mary's baby was one year old, Florence brought him a gift of baby chicks in varied Easter colors. Florence could always think of dear things to do at just the right time, though so quietly they were almost unnoticed. She was always there when friends and loved ones needed her. In those young days of their lives, couples close to the Rossis were often rejoicing in a new baby's coming. And inevitably Florence called at the home with a love-prompted gift for the child.

But, in the midst of all their zeal for church and the new business, Anthony and Florence were to be sorely tested. Florence began a brave battle with serious heart trouble. And so suddenly the unthinkable happened. Only one week after taking the baby chicks to one-year-old Charles, Florence became critically ill. Rushed to Larabee Hospital with a heart attack, no room was available. With her bed in the hallway, Anthony holding her hand, they repeated the Twenty-third Psalm together. Moments later, Anthony's beloved companion, his Florence, slipped away. It was April 21, 1951.

At home now Anthony was alone except for his faithful dog, Lady. In the daytime Mary took care of the empty house, more resolved than ever to do what she could for Mr. Rossi. Grief turned to fervor to keep the house as Florence wanted it to be. She cooked a hot meal daily for his lunch, and often he would bring a friend with him. Mary also saw to it that something tasty was on the stove for him when he came home for supper.

Anthony now gave himself more than ever to the business. It was a total effort. He knew what he wanted in quality, volume, and lowest cost to customers. But the how-to kept his creative mind concentrating on building the equipment and machines to do the job. Tropicana demanded of him long hours into the night, often all night at the plant.

Vying with Tropicana, Anthony had another consuming interest: studying the Bible. Friends met at his home on his free evenings and his house was open to them at anytime. No doors were locked. With his friends, debating was stimulating mental exercise. They confronted various angles of theology, searching for truth. Some brought books and commentaries. But Anthony and Murray (Kesten) insisted that they stick with the Bible itself. Anthony reminded everyone of how he first discovered Christ through reading the Bible in the New York City Library.

Then, all in need of guidance, they learned of a Bible class in Sarasota. Doug Bell explained it to Anthony. "Tony, it is taught by a very lovely lady. Her name is Mrs. William Northen. She explains things so that you can understand."

"A woman teacher?" Anthony held back.

"She's really great, Tony, very warm and cordial. And does she know the Bible!"

"All right, Doug, I'll go. At least once."

This Bible study would become the watershed for Anthony's concept of the Christian message. An evening came when he accepted Doug Bell's invitation to attend the Sarasota Bible study.

Impose on God?

DOUG BELL DROVE his car with spirit. He was that kind of a person. By now they were with the go signal at the old Ringling Hotel, Sarasota. Curving to the left he continued south on Tamiami Trail. Anthony and Doug were talking together fervently, as they had been since Doug picked up his friend in Bradenton.

"Tony," Doug asked with challenge, "if you died tonight would you be sure you were going to heaven?"

Anthony hesitated. Then, in a low, confidential voice, he answered, "Doug, you know I hope so. I try to please God. All my life I have wanted to do his will. But how can I impose on God to say he should receive me in heaven? How can anyone know that?"

"Well, Tony, this class we're headed for tonight is just for you. The teacher is the finest, Mrs. Northen."

"You told me that. I am surprised to hear the teacher is a woman." Anthony sounded dubious.

"Yes, you will love her. She is an older lady and charming. She really knows the Bible. Just now she is teaching us from the book of Romans. I promise, Tony, she will convince you that a person can know with certainty that he is a child of God with a home in heaven."

By this time they had come to Prospect Street and turned right going into Osprey South. Presently came the two pillars at the entrance to North Harbor Drive. In no time they were parking, along with many other cars, in front of the large gray home.

"This is where Dr. Hugh Reaves and his wife Sally live. They have a spacious living room and also a long veranda facing the canal. So many are attending the class now that we need this space."

Doug fairly sprinted to the door with his big "Mr. Trop-icana" close behind.

"Well, Tony," sang Sally Reaves. "We are so delighted to see you! You and Doug are just in time! Come, let's find a seat."

"Sally Reaves is a lovely hostess," thought Anthony. They were given seats near the front of a larger three-deep circle of people. Everyone had his Bible open to the book of Romans. Anthony noticed Peggy and Murray Keston were present. Also, behind him, were Nettie and Jim Pratt.

"So many of our friends are here," Anthony noticed. Across from where he sat were Harry and Martha Evelyn Parham and the Hallet Hullingers.

As the class began, Anthony liked the teacher at once. She was dainty, soft-spoken and gracious—a southern lady with a charming accent and winning personality. Mrs. Northen reached out to each one present with kindness and understanding. She was convinced herself of the truth she taught and could lead her class to see the book for themselves, to discover its application to their lives. Using Donald Gray Barnhouse's *Rightly Dividing the Word of Truth,* she underscored the meaning of the verses as she had her class read and follow the logic of the text.

"Therefore, being justified by faith, we have peace with God" (Rom 5:1 KJV).

"For the wages of sin is death; but the gift of God is eternal life through Jesus Christ our Lord" (Rom 6:23 KJV).

People were free to ask questions. Doug spoke out. "Mrs. Northen, how can a person be sure he is a child of God? When can one be assured of heaven?"

Mrs. Northen replied by pointing from text to text in a fully convincing exposition. She showed them how God accepted each one according to his decision to sincerely receive Christ. Repenting of one's sins first, of course, one confesses Christ as Lord and believes in his heart that God has raised Christ from the dead. "See, this is what Romans 10:9-10 plainly states to us."

Mrs. Northen discussed with them Paul's magnificent treatise on salvation by grace through faith.

Anthony was astonished. Looking at the very words he needed to understand, he was persuaded. "Not in my merit, but in the worthiness of Christ—this is my promise, my assurance. Heaven then, is the destiny of one who truly receives Christ." He saw so clearly the words, "There is therefore now no condemnation to them which are in Christ

Jesus" (Rom 8:1 KJV).

It had seemed only minutes, yet the class was over. "Come back next Friday evening and we will study more together," Mrs. Northen was saying. A warm stir of greetings and goodbyes were soon past.

Doug and Anthony, back in the car, spun along northward to Bradenton. "Now, do you see, Tony? You can be sure—and me too—that you are going to heaven, that you are God's child."

"Yes, Doug. You know she said, 'When you are born into God's family, you can't be unborn. God may need to spank you at times, but once you are his, you are sure of his salvation.' "

"Yes, Tony, it is not because of what we are or do, but because of who Christ is and what he has done for us."

The lighted signs on the highway accented the shining joy in Anthony's heart. Understanding the message of Romans was like flying.

"My feet won't touch ground for at least a week!" he laughed.

The Bible study in Sarasota became a must for him as well as for many of his friends. They listened, and faith took hold to make all the difference in their lives.

Doug volunteered, both he and Marge, to go to Africa as missionaries. Harry Parham became a preacher, as did Hallet Hullinger. Others lifted the standard of their witness within the occupations they pursued. Anthony renewed his zeal to expand Tropicana and found he could use monetary means to forward God's work, to encourage missionaries in their service. He now had two dominant spiritual motives, to live close to God day by day and to be useful in God's work in the world.

Then, one day, without warning, Doug Bell suddenly left his earthly witness for heaven. He died of a heart attack before he could ever reach Africa. But his many friends would cherish his open testimony for the Lord. Every memory of him prodded them to follow his example of articulate fervent faith. Anthony would never forget that most important conversation with Doug, and its sequel. He could still hear his directive, "Mrs. Northen teaches the Word as one who knows the Author." No wonder the group of Bradenton young couples discovered faith in its bright daylight of understanding and knew life for each of them had found a significant new beginning.

For Anthony Rossi, at this time, had accepted Jesus Christ as his own Savior and Lord. Born again? He was sure of it.

Papá

T HE PROPELLORS ON the Israeli airplane whirred with the trans-Atlantic night. Out of New York two hours earlier, the flight was to land at Rome in the morning. Every seat was filled. Many Jewish passengers were headed for Israel. Nearly everyone was settled down under a blanket to rest. Supper had been served and cleared. Conversation simmered down to a whisper here and there.

Anthony Rossi, in a seat near the window framing a velvet black sky, was too alert for sleep. He snapped on the light above his head and opened a book—*the* book. Lost in the marvel of the Epistle to the Romans, he read thoughtfully through the swift hours humming toward dawn.

He was enroute to Italy, to Sicily, with a keen purpose. "I must share this message with all my brothers and sisters. They will listen, I believe. But I don't know how to approach father. Who am I to try to instruct such a revered person? How can I appropriately explain these things to him?"

By this year, 1952, Anthony's father, much respected in the city of Messina, was in his eighty-second year. Anthony prayed, "Lord, give me wisdom. Show me what to say, how to begin."

The night had begun to gray as Anthony drifted into shallow sleep. When his small window let in shafts of sunlight, he woke up.

"Where am I?" He rubbed his eyes. Israelis were in the aisle, at prayers, wearing their round caps and phylacteries on arms and foreheads.

Anthony sat up. With a rush the realization flooded his consciousness, "We are almost to Rome."

There, he met his brother Constantino with his wife Sandra and their tiny daughter Anna. Together they scrambled aboard the southbound train to Reggio and the Messina Straits. Then by ferry-crossing on the train, they reached the depot at Messina.

The family, warm and jovial, smothered him with salutations. Papá, a large man at more than six feet, had white hair and goatee now along with his handlebar mustache—so intriguing to a grandchild on his knee. He was a great lover of children. His long arms strongly embraced his son from America. Nino, about his size, had been away for more than twenty years. The little girls, Elvira and Teresa, were now grown and married with their own children in their teens. The brothers Carlo and Salvatore with their families, pressed in to be next to hug him. And Alfredo, still single, gave fervent greetings in his deep basso. Zia Tina, the buxom stepmother gave him a happy welcome-hug also.

Nino was overwhelmed emotionally by the joyous encounter with everyone at once. "So much I have to tell them," he pondered. Some already knew about his ambition to get fresh-chilled orange juice on the American breakfast table. But the more important news was that salvation is by grace through faith alone. Good works and walking in obedience must follow, proving faith to be real, but good works alone were not the route to peace with God.

But attempts to share this insight did not go well. He tried to talk to each of his brothers and sisters, one at a time. Each thought of an urgent errand and was suddenly out of reach. They were all afraid to touch the subject that dominated Nino's mind. "One day I know each one of them will discover what I have learned. I shall not give up until they do."

The hour came when the entire family gathered for Pranza. Papá sat at the head of the long table. Nino, in the place of privilege was seated at his right. In a pause before they were served, Nino suddenly addressed his father.

"Papá, will it be good if we first thank the Lord for bringing us all safely together again?"

"Why yes, son. A good thing. You pray." Simply, revealing an intimate relationship with God, Anthony closed saying, "I pray in the name of Jesus Christ, my Savior."

When everyone lifted his head, Nino looked at Papá. The old gentleman's eyes were moist with feeling. "Son," he said, "from now on I will pray in the name of Jesus Christ, my Savior."

How quiet, how instant, the working of the Holy Spirit! "Papá understands," Nino marveled, thinking, "God has heard my prayer. How good that I came!"

The Burnout

I AM SORRY, TONY."

In the dark hours of the morning, May 1954, Johnny Douglas stood with Anthony outside the white wood-frame office building at Tropicana. The air was acrid and the haze of the big fire still choked the place. Anthony, six feet two inches tall, looked down into the face of his staunch team-mate, Johnny. He was one of the score of hand-picked officers of the company, each with his own gift to use in all-out effort. Murray Kesten took charge of purchasing, David Hamrick at quality control, plus a long list of the finest sort of men, committed to lead in their churches and dedicated to Tropicana's citrus industry. It could, it must, develop into the largest manufacturer of fresh-chilled orange and grape-fruit juice—the best in the world! Early on, Tropicana became known as the Christian orange juice company.

"Well, Johnny, we can thank the Lord that no one was in the building. It burned so quickly, yet not one person was hurt."

That evening had begun as a gala occasion—Tropicana's first annual dinner party for all eight hundred employees and their spouses. Tables were loaded with gourmet food—plenty for all. They celebrated the brand-new cold storage building, completed except for the cold storage equipment to be installed the next day. Three blocks square it stood, white, impressive. Beside it was the first cold storage warehouse, packed tight with citrus products ready for transport. Only a fire wall separated the two buildings.

The great room rumbled with the happy sounds of banqueting—a time for fun and laughter, comical entertaining and excellent food. Toasts, speeches, singing and music lengthened the fiesta on into the evening. Guests seated under the lights and festive decorations could not have dreamed that their roof, freshly tarred today, was steadily smoldering red hot and spreading end to end.

At last the dinner party dissolved as folks said unhurried goodbyes. After a while the last carful of them passed through the company gates. They could see with the outdoor lighting the fleet of large refrigerator trucks all set to be loaded with cartoned juice to go out tomorrow for an ever-widening market. The fresh-chilled juice had become popular instantly. And Anthony, with characteristic foresight, long ago placed his order for one million dollars worth of trucks. He did this even before machinery for the juice processing was yet in place because he was convinced of its success. And sure enough, when orders for orange juice avalanched, he was prepared. It was now, "Go Tropicana, Go."

By eleven o'clock the annual Tropicana festival had ended. They were a family company, working together as friends. Mundane jobs of weighing, washing, inspecting, packaging were transformed into a dream being fulfilled in unison. "A great evening!" they all said with mutual feeling.

Then, by spontaneous combustion the roof of the new building exploded into flames. Those leaping, hungry flames soared into a tide of fire across the top of the building. The burning tar ascended into a blackrolling column of smoke, spiraling high into the midnight sky. People in Bradenton, Palmetto and even as far south as Sarasota's northern limits could see it—orange and black, wicked against the horizon.

After several eternal minutes sirens screamed and firefighters converged from all directions. Every available firefighting truck raced to meet this emergency.

"Save the storage building next door!" The chief had many voices. Men scrambled to the top of the fire wall, wetting it down with hoses and gunning the flames with the force of water. Even Anthony's pastor, Rev. Thad Entzminger appeared on that wall, aiming a fire hose at the diabolical blaze. Help rushed in from everywhere. Some relayed buckets of water to the burning building.

At last, the fighters won. The flames staggered, collapsed and expired. A charred shell of the new cold storage plant yet stood. Its concrete block walls were intact, but bare. The entire roof and flooring had been consumed; a half-million dollars lost in the burnout.

But Anthony Rossi could smile through tears when Johnny said, "I'm sorry." "Johnny, I think God has decided to make Tropicana a great company. Now it is my job to keep working hard and thinking too, praying all the time." They walked together to their cars parked near the office building close to Tropicana's entrance. They were the last to leave the office while within the humming factories farther away, the night shift kept at their jobs.

Anthony spoke again with conviction. "Johnny, with all our refrigerated trucks, we are still not able to handle the volume we need. The demand for Tropicana orange juice is more than our transport capabilities."

"I'm thinking now of a ship! It can carry two million gallons of orange juice in bulk, enough to supply New York and New England markets for each week."

Johnny gasped. The lamppost next to his car revealed how wide his eyes were. He had no words.

They got into their cars and drove out the gate. But one of them, maybe both (because hope is catching), moved forward into the dark that was just before the dawn.

The S.S. Tropicana

T HE LONG ISLAND PIER at Whitestone in Queens County, New York, stood vacant. Thick knotty boards were gray like the horizon. No ship in sight. It was Tuesday, February 19, 1957. Anthony Rossi, wearing a gray herringbone topcoat open over his dark suit, watched tensely. He took out his pocket watch. It was already 12:30 P.M. The East River, a wrinkled gray, like the pewter sky close upon it, flowed more frowning than buoyant on that mediocre day. In contrast, Anthony's heartbeat was ecstatic with hope and suspense.

The S.S. Tropicana, a tanker of fresh-chilled orange juice from Florida was due for its first time at exactly one o'clock.

Albert Stark, now vice president in charge of the ship, stepped out of the Tropicana plant building and walked over to the pier. He had a message for his brother-in-law. Anthony's hopeful smile slackened. "Say, Anthony, New York Port authorities have just telephoned. There isn't a chance for the ship to get here before evening."

Anthony knew by heart the route of the ship. It must enter the lower harbor and go up the East River, then, just a mile from this pier, the S. S. Tropicana had to go through a monumental hazard to mariners called Hellgate. "They can't get through the Hellgate until the tide changes," Albert moaned.

Anthony thought of the 450 guests filling the big carton storage room of the New York plant. The Brass Rail caterers had turned it into a festive banquet hall with lavish buffet from hors d'oeuvres through desserts. Coffee was fresh roasted, and Brass Rail Virginia baked ham could not be rivaled, nor their snow-white cheese cakes and fresh butter cookies with other imported delicacies and gift baskets. Most visitors had arrived by now and the place was buzzing with observers who had come to welcome the S.S. Tropicana on her maiden voyage.

Two and a half days earlier, amid fanfare and even international publicity, the ship sailed from Port Canaveral. "The Golden Stream," as they called it in Florida, had become a mammoth undertaking.

First of all, finding the right port site was remarkable. That twenty-one acre spot was the only possibility on Florida's Atlantic coast for such a project. The property fronted on a thirty-five-foot-deep inlet leading to the ocean on one end and an inland waterway on the west. This inlet protected Canaveral harbor from rough seas.

The $5,000,000 plant, rapidly constructed, had nine buildings including a cold storage structure measuring 1,500,000 square feet—the longest one in the South. It required forty-three carloads of insulation and 480 tons of refrigeration.

"The Golden Stream" of liquid sunshine poured from pipes into enormous stainless steel tanks, and from those through pipes into the ship tanks aboard.

Anthony Rossi's innovation startled the citrus industry of Florida. Many were doubters. "Plumb crazy!" they warned. This evaluation of the enterprise influenced some New York bankers to politely refuse loans to the company for the idea.

The ship's tanks, because of their size, were built in sections ashore in Lakeland, Florida. They were cut apart in order to hoist them into the hold of the 8,000-ton cargo ship purchased from the United Fruit Company. Rossi had bought the Cape Avinof for $650,000. Her Captain Smith chose to remain with the ship as it would be transformed into the S.S. Tropicana.

After loading the tanks, craftsmen reassembled and welded them to the hold-deck with specialized insulation and bracing to allow for temperature changes. A network of stainless steel pipes allowed the six tanks to be filled individually. Carefully planned, the system would preserve the freshness and flavor of the juice, as well as its purity.

"But it will never work!" cried the doubters. Noisy words buffeted the Tropicana team, but no negatives could dissuade them.

"The juice is sure to spoil in two and a half days at sea," the hecklers added.

Yet, by Anthony Rossi's detailed calculations, this dream was not impossible. He was confident.

Newspeople gloried in the story. "The orange juice will be carried in six huge stainless steel tanks and when the S.S.

Tropicana sails, it will be the first time fresh-squeezed fluid orange juice has ever been moved in volume by sea."

To those closest to him, Anthony explained the venture, "I have been thinking a long time about the need to transport the juice in volume we are targeting for the northeast. Early morning, before dawn, I am awake, thinking. I pray to God about this. Then the idea develops in my mind. I believe God gave it to me."

"Then, at Tropicana, we drew the plans and worked out the idea." "But how did you ever accomplish this—an orange juice tanker?" some still asked.

Anthony, a little surprised at their incredulity, answered, "The work we did is just the result of using our own common sense." It all seemed that simple to him!

The tanks on the ship had 6 1/2" of foam-glass insulation to maintain 28 degrees to 30 degrees temperature during the voyage. In addition to this, Rossi had already developed the freezing of slabs of pure juice, three-feet square, four-inches thick. From the cold storage plant in Canaveral, these slabs went through grinding machines and then into the ship, chilling the volume of juice to 28 degrees.

Today, scanning the East River, Anthony mused, "Of course, I never studied engineering. So how could I know this could not be done?"

He had not been afraid to take the risk, but even a carefully planned one, cost him a total of about $10,000,000. Financing it through the company profits and bank loans, he had thrown everything into this venture.

Some asked, "Will the ship transport divert volume from the Bradenton operation?"

"No," Rossi pointed out, "we are getting new dairies every day and expect greater volume out of Bradenton than we had last year." At this date, Tropicana produced more chilled juice than all other Florida companies combined. "We have reached our present leading position on quality and service," Rossi told a news analyst. "And through this new method we intend to improve both."

"But is it not too great an expense to use the ship?" reporters questioned. Again, the answer. "The ship carries 1,450,000 gallons every trip. This amount of juice, cartoned and trucked, costs $250,000 plus an additional $15,000 for loading. The S.S. Tropicana will deliver this same amount for only $15,000."

Whitestone guests were becoming restless; Anthony noted the time at five minutes to one o'clock. "Should I tell the caterers to go ahead with serving?"

The New York plant pipelines and series of twelve-foot-diameter receiving tanks were ready for the orange juice to be pumped from the ship. Lines of cartons on their conveyor belts were assembled to be filled, 140 quart cartons a minnute. Trucks were ready to deliver the product to the dairies in New York, New England and Pennsylvania.

Minutes slowly circled the watch in Anthony's hand. But wait! There is a white dot on the horizon, rapidly enlarging. A majestic sight, the bow of the ship rose up, snow white against the low-hung sky. The S.S. Tropicana had made it. A few more minutes. Then, at precisely one o'clock, she swung alongside the splintery boards of the dock platform. Guests swarmed to touch her. Bill and Bob of Bradenton, Florida, were there to take the pictures.

The ship was decorated with a line of streamers from bow to high mast to rear mast and stern.

"Captain Smith," Anthony greeted him fervently, "they said you couldn't make the Hellgate!"

"But," the Captain exploded, "didn't you tell me to be here on the point of one o'clock today?"

"How did you do it?"

"Well, Mr. Rossi, I know this place and every hazard of it. I've taken this ship through Hellgate many times. I just didn't bother to stop for a tugboat. We're here!"

After the christening ceremony, when Margaret Donnally in bathing suit broke a carton of orange juice against the ship's hull, the guests were served juice from the ship to taste. Some with trembling hands lifted paper cups to their lips. Would it be sour? They sipped it. "Good. Wonderful. Fresh as from the orange!" Sunshine was in this juice on the gray-weather day. On came the sumptuous buffet. Later, the same room was changed to a conference hall for the meeting that followed.

Headlines pronounced the S.S. Tropicana a "dramatic fast-growing phase of merchandising Florida citrus."

A new era in the marketing of liquid sunshine began that day.

Chiesa Bibbia Cristiana

THE S.S. TROPICANA fulfilled Anthony's expectations. The New York markets were booming, and so the company that began with his small investment of $15,000 had now become his giant brainchild, absorbing heart and mind. And his hand-picked choice team, each an expert in his field, worked in an aura of excitement. Anthony schemed constantly of how to improve the production, how to move forward. And move forward they did, to take the far lead in citrus marketing.

Yet paralleling the business was an even deeper interest—God's work. How to do more to impact missions. Well informed on world conditions, Anthony prayed to be of significant use to God in vital and constructive enterprises. Also, he resolved, "If I ever marry again, my wife must be a missionary." Eight years had passed since Florence died—years spent alone. Even the German Shepherd, Lady, had succumbed to old age.

And it came to pass that Anthony did pluck his new wife out of the mainstream of missions to become his partner in serving the Lord. Anthony married Sanna Morrison Barlow in London, England, on September 11, 1954. She had returned to London from her work assignment in South Africa. They decided on a wedding in England because they would go immediately to Italy. Anthony was thinking of his own homeland as his first missionary goal. "We must see a church established in Messina!" This purpose would not be let go until the Rossis saw it become a fact.

"First, I want to introduce my own people to Jesus Christ and to all he can mean to us in our present lives, as well as for our future in heaven."

The Rossis flew from London to Rome. There brother Constantino and his wife Sandra lived. *Incontevale* was Sandra—charming, delightful. Her English acquired in university became a communication bridge for the new Mrs. Anthony Rossi.

Tino linked arms with Nino and they together enjoyed sightseeing with their spouses, Sandra and Sanna. *Roma,* the eternal city, was fabulous.

However, touring faded into background trivia when Nino would open his Italian Bible and read to everyone from the book of John. Tino and Sandra found their Bibles, and Sanna also was given a Gospel of John in Italian. She found the musical Italian more sparkling than Latin, more lyrical than English. Like the Bereans of first-century church history,

Tino and Sandra eagerly searched the Scriptures, asking questions and savoring Nino's explanations. Conversation centered on these truths from God's Word.

Then, following a panorama of beautiful Italia by train to Messina a few days later, the two pairs of Talamo-Rossis were hailed at the depot by that plaintive four-tone whistle of the family clan. Brothers and sisters with their families stormed the train compartment and pulled down luggage. The Roma Rossis could scarcely gather up their hand luggage.

After an exuberant welcome and an introduction to their hotel rooms where sail boats were only a stone's throw away, Sandra and Tino, Sanna and Nino were feted at the beautiful home of Anthony's older brother Carlo and Ida, his vivacious and gracious wife.

When some days had slipped by, Nino first approached Carlo for permission to have a circle of Bible reading in his home. Carlo politely insisted he could not change his religion. But Nino countered, "Carlo, *per favore,* we will just read from your own Bible. It is such a wonderful book! I want you to understand it better. We will learn together." Thus it was that family Bible studies occupied evening time, as sure as the previous festive meal together.

Every September the Anthony Rossis took their vacation in Italy. The home Bible studies were the essential purpose of those visits. The family circle grew to include friends. Then, a new thing. Nino planned for a first public gathering for Bible exposition in the summer of 1966. It was preceded by months of advertising and much study and preparation by Anthony in Bradenton, Florida.

When Anthony arrived by plane from the United States, all was ready. The hall rented for the five-day conference was furnished with piano, pulpit and seating for more than two hundred people. However, a nephew had warned him ahead of time that perhaps no one would come, not in cathedraled Messina, not in Sicily.

But when Anthony ascended the stairs and opened the door to the assembly hall, he was astounded. There sat at least two hundred and fifty people waiting. He was to speak to them, and he was scared.

Holding his notes in trembling hands, he began to explain his subject simply. "Why did Christ come into the world?" Telling the love of God in Christ soon became a joy that no stage fright could squelch. "We have come here to assure you that God loves you and that we love you."

After five evenings, the businessman-turned-preacher saw twenty-four persons courageous enough to walk up to the platform and publicly attest their trust in Christ as Savior. Here was the first breakthrough—such a thin wedge in Messina's multitudes. Yet twenty-four, most of them from Anthony's own family, were indeed a tiny nucleus of the church that had begun.

Through their yearly September visits to Sicily, the Rossis watched the Messina church develop. Nine more conferences followed this first one. They were held in a suitable hall of the *fiera,* or exposition center, adjoining Villa Mazzini on the waterfront.

Sometimes Dr. Stephen Olford was speaker with his able interpreter Elio Milazzo from Florence, Italy.[2] At other times Dr. Mariano Di Gangi, speaking his own mother tongue, taught fellow Sicilians.[3] They heard him earnestly. His message came through with splendid clarity and power. Today Di Gangi visits the church in Messina once a year.

In late afternoon, preceding the evening service at the

fiera, Anthony always spoke to the people gathering in the seaside park, Villa Mazzini. With Anthony were Fritz and Veneta Liechti with their junior-age boys and girls—all singing with guitar accompaniment. Many people were attracted by their music. And to the crowd encircling them, Anthony Rossi, in his boyhood setting, talked to the people about his discovery of the Bible and what it reveals of the love of God in Christ. His witness was sincere, winsome, magnetic.

As late shadows spread to twilight and the park lights came on, Anthony closed his remarks, and warmly urged his audience to follow him to the *fiera* only a few steps away. The white gate to the white exposition building was open. The assembly hall was beginning to fill up. Many also followed Anthony, a pied piper happy to bring in newcomers along behind him.

The Messina church grew through the years, deepening its roots, increasing its membership. Today (1986) Chiesa Bibbia Cristiana maintains a congregation of more then two hundred, filling their sanctuary on Viale Europa in the center of Messina. The church operates a Christian radio ministry twenty-four hours a day. Rev. John Gilmore with his wife Maureen and children, Jonathan and Debbie, are a dedicated team, working together for the church. It is Jonathan, now in his twenties, who directs the radio ministry. Public response to radio keeps the church phone ringing and draws visitors to the Sunday services.

And at this time the Messina church stands tall. It is alive, and it is salt in the city, the ancient city, for Messina dates back to the eighth century B.C. Chiesa Bibbia Cristiana, filled with young people as well as old, is a loving family, a steadfast witness of inestimable value on Messina's Viale Europa today.

At Point Pleasant on the Manatee

LIGHT DIMLY SHONE from the alarm clock in their bedroom. The Rossis woke up promptly and dressed in joyful haste. Sanna pulled the draperies on the wide north windows open. At their boat-dock on the northwest corner of their lot, both could see the yacht. "She's there already!" Anthony's voice was jubilant. "The skipper has the Miss Tropicana waiting for us."

In their large living room, the Rossis stopped a minute on the way to the kitchen. To the east, pouring obliquely through the glass doors, dawn was golden-red over the Green Bridge and behind the city pier on the point just east of their own. They turned to look west, since the room was all windows. The Manatee River widened here to spread out into Tampa Bay about eight miles away. The water had a satin sheen, reflecting some of the dawn colors like a vast mirror of morning. A glorious day!

Anthony then hurried to the kitchen, his wife following. "I have only three hours to spare, you know, from seven o'clock to ten. But it's a great day for the fishing trip!"

In less than fifteen minutes, they had prepared breakfast to carry out to the waiting boat. Their guests were up early too. Visitors always liked the colors given to the silver river from the circling sky.

Dr. and Mrs. Stanley Soltau, veteran missionaries of Korea, were now in charge of a large church in Memphis, Tennessee. "What a privilege to have the Soltaus with us," the Rossis thought in unison.

"Good morning!" Dr. Soltau and Molly entered the kitchen as the Rossis were about to carry breakfast and picnic plates out to the little ship. Molly's smile spoke of the day's joy. And the twinkle in her husband's eyes also foretold the fun in store for everyone this morning.

The tide was right for easily boarding the yacht steady in its place at the dock. Below deck, the neat cabin with its permanent table and chairs became their breakfast nook. Scrambled eggs, bacon, Danish pastry, and coffee were still hot. And Tropicana orange juice accented the menu as liquid sunshine must.

The skipper steered the 50-foot Miss Tropicana along the deeper channel of the river, carving a single white wake across the surface.

By the time breakfasting was over, the boat skimmed into the Tampa Bay. Out beyond the bay rolled the Gulf of Mexico that laced its surf along the white sand shores of Anna Maria Island.

The two couples bounded up to top deck and immediately the two men took to their fishing rods. Anthony wondered if they were in for the usual bore of fruitless patience. The skipper anchored Miss Tropicana right under an umbrella of blue sky. All around, though, were veils of mist and light cloud falling softly upon the water—an enchanting scene.

"Ohh!" all exclaimed as one. Near the ship, mackerel were leaping in silver arcs out of the bay. At the bow of the boat, a school of porpoise somersaulted, blowing spray as they rolled and rollicked—the sleek gray curve of their backs surfacing frequently.

"Look!" Molly's lovely face, crowned with prematurely white hair, expressed this moment's gladness. She pointed south and east. Out there, quite apart from the other, soft scarves of sky fell touching the sea, and rain squalls so narrow as though from a watering pot, poured into small circles below.

"Rainbows!" Everybody saw them. They arched across the mists and showers in vivid colors. Double tokens of blessing.

Nearly everywhere fish surfaced as sea birds swooped and screamed, catching fish in their beaks. Pelicans in particular soared highest, then upending themselves beaks first, plummeted into the frenetic circles of minnows, always coming up with a large mackerel or mullet to gulp alive and whole.

Anthony and Stanley Soltau cast out their lines. No waiting this morning. Instantly their rods bowed, and a large catch challenged the fisherman's skill. And then another one. "This is a beauty." More—then more. Buckets soon filled with flipping fish.

The ladies chose to just watch the fishing, and to breathe in deeply those heaven-on-earth hours. They all were in a world apart—Anthony from Tropicana office routine, and his wife and guests from more everyday activities of shopping or errands in town.

Out here on a crystal sea, this morning seemed melded to the sky in awesome harmony.

Anthony pulled in his twelfth fish, another large mackerel. But, as he began to dislodge it from the hook, the fish caught his finger. Bandaids were handy since Miss Tropicana was equipped for first aid. Then everyone, first assured no real damage was done, gave way to laughter. Dr. Soltau responded with his irrepressible wit saying, "Anthony, I have always expected a fish to bite the hook. This is the first time I ever saw a fish bite the fisherman!"

Both beauty and gaity had framed three unforgettable hours.

By ten o'clock the Soltaus and Rossis were back home. They would remember this early morning that touched the joy their Creator has written into His design for blessing and celebration of life.

The Mexican Pride

I N THE FALL OF 1963, Florida's orange groves promised abundance. Tropicana, still leading the chilled juice industry, geared itself to handle maximum volume in 1964. Then, without warning, a steel fist of cold weather drove deep into Florida and gripped the land with a hard and long freeze. Smudge pots and burning rubber tires failed, with all other efforts, to forestall the worst hard freeze ever. TV weather channels photographed disaster. News came by telephone before dawn. The golden harvest promised was over and yesterday's bright prospects had failed.

Rossi caught the swift challenge with a thumping heart. The day following, Tropicana officers gathered at the con-

ference table with their leader. "What *can* we do?" Obvious-
ly Florida could not yield an adequate supply of fresh fruit.
"Go to juice made with concentrate from Brazil," some advised.

"Never!" countered the boss. "Our product is 100% pure
fresh-chilled juice. We cannot change." Nor would he give
into failure. More inquiry pointed to Mexico. Plenty of fine
juice oranges were there and their groves were glad for a
buyer like Tropicana.

This meant setting up office and facilities at Mexico's port
of Tuxpan in the Gulf. Within a very few days, Murray and
Peggy Kesten went to Tuxpan and directed the Tropicana
operation there, along with others from the company helping.

At first, oranges were tumbled into huge baskets, passed
through fumigation and shipped by freighters to Florida.
This seemed to be working. Tropicana factory went full
speed ahead.

However, on about the third cargo of oranges, a state
inspector thought he noticed some evidence of the Mexican
fruit fly. Hence, no more oranges could be brought into
Florida from Mexico.

Again the Company was in a dilemma. And the reconstituted juice idea surfaced. It was decidedly squelched.

Rossi had a new plan. "If we can't bring Mexico oranges
into Florida, we will bring the orange juice itself."

"How?"

And the Tropicana team of gifted men were taken by
surprise at what the boss had already thought through in
detail.

Late one evening, the Rossis took their houseguests, Dr.
and Mrs. Allen Fleece, to see a barge at Port Sutton south of

Tampa. The fifty-foot-wide old hulk looked grim in the darkness there. But not to Anthony Rossi. He could see it transformed and knew how to direct every phase of that metamorphasis.

Sure enough, only three months later, the old tub became "The Mexican Pride." Now seaworthy, it headed for the Mexico port. El Toro, the tugboat, towed the floating juice factory safely to Tuxpan.

By March 23, the Mexican Pride off Tuxpan began to process the sweet Mexican oranges. The fruit came aboard the boat factory on huge conveyor belts. Headlines picked up the novel enterprise proclaiming the operation to be "The first floating factory of its kind." Now Tropicana-on-sea could move its factory to any place oranges could be found.

But near the dock at Tuxpan was a busy highway. How could so many oranges be continuously trundled across it and on to the Mexican Pride?

Rossi, often on the scene himself at Tuxpan, came up with the solution to dig a tunnel under the highway. And again the prefix fell from the word "impossible." By conveyors, the large volume of oranges were shunted through the tunnel and rolled on to the processing deck of the ship.

The Pride resembled a huge houseboat. Boilers, extractors and other necessary processing equipment were located on top deck along with quality control laboratories. On second deck was the refrigerated storage tank capable of holding 225,000 gallons of orange juice. Second deck also held sleeping quarters for officers and crew, offices, dining room and kitchen. On third deck, the generators installed had fifty per cent reserve power.

Orange juice was automatically processed then pumped from the mother ship's tank to a 205-foot-long converted

L.C.M. barge which would take it directly to Florida's west coast. The juice could remain at thirty-two degrees in the ten-inch-thick insulated tanks. For more than fifteen days it would keep and still be perfect.

Two L.C.M. barges with their tugboats operated on a fixed schedule to and from Mexico. When the first barge pulled in, newsmen were there to pick up headlines. "175,000 gallons of fresh orange juice, the first ever processed at sea, arrived in Florida Thursday. Another first for the firm."

From the barge, the chilled juice was pumped into sterile tank trucks on the ready at Port Sutton. In about an hour, they delivered the immaculately sterile juice in volume to Tropicana's bottling area. This operation was carried out under the eye of the federal Food and Drug Administration, and it was successful. The taste and quality were perfect.

In addition to the Port Sutton to Bradenton transport, Tropicana owned a fleet of pineapple freighters, often docked at the pier in downtown Bradenton. Mexico pineapple added zest to the fruit salads, and some were juiced for a new orange-pineapple drink. These larger ships docked at the yacht basin on the Manatee became a favorite interest for local artists and photographers.

This innovative transport from Tuxpan to Bradenton lasted one year. But when Florida's groves were full of fruit once more, and Mexico began to push up the price of oranges, Rossi judged it best to send his floating factory away. One night it silently departed from Tuxpan's dock, and the magic industry there vanished. The processor barge, like the ship from Canaveral to New York, closed its story.

For Tropicana's chief was ever flexible and farsighted. Already on his desk were newer ideas, better quality products and distribution yet to come.

The Decorator Machine

MURRAY," ANTHONY looked up at his good friend, Keston, the buyer for Tropicana, "these machines just won't do."

"Best on the market, Tony."

"Yes, but they don't silk-screen fast enough to decorate our bottles. Send them back."

"Oh, then what will we do?"

"We'll think about it. God will give an answer."

A night or so later, Anthony was in a deep sleep. It was the time everyone slept, around 2:30 or 3 A.M. He dreamed his favorite dream. He was flying over obstacles, over precipices, and he was free. Nothing could be impossible. In his dreams, he loved to fly—high in the starlit atmosphere. Then at about 4 A.M. he became conscious in a substantive, creative sort of way. First thoughts were prayers. "No time is so wonderful as that in which I am in communion with my God," his spirit told him. "God loves me." He knew it. "And all God does is for my own good." Prayers gathered into focus.

"Dear Lord, you could help me to understand how we can have a decorator machine that is right for *us.*" Precise coordination was involved as the glass furnace dropped liquid flame into a mold. Seconds later, the mold released a perfect quart size bottle to keep pace in single file along the conveyor belt. Timing had to be exact.

"The only machine we know of will decorate forty bottles per minute. We need, at the speed we are moving the bottles to the juicing tap, at least 300 per minute."

Thinking. Thinking. Dawn softly approached and through the bedroom's west windows light filtered in, bringing chairs and dressers into distinct and solid form.

But it wasn't quite time to get up. A new idea had just begun to intrigue Anthony's mind. As the clock ticked, his mind clicked off the action of an imaginary silk-screening machine. The bottles must swing into a rotating route. But he didn't quite have it.

By now it was time for prayers on a more conscious level. As these closed, he and his wife recited the Twenty-third Psalm together.

For Anthony, the time taken to dress and shave couldn't be wasted either. He turned on his record player to chapters of the Bible read by Alexander Scorby.

At breakfast, the Rossis were silent. Anthony was thinking deeply. After breakfast, they read devotions from Spurgeon's

"Morning and Evening" and two or three Psalms, plus the one chapter marked for the day's reading through the Bible. Anthony then led in closing prayer, looking to God to make it a worthwhile one in His sight.

This day, however, he did not hurry to the front hall closet to get his coat and head out for Tropicana. Instead, he sat down in one of their two large tapestry chairs. His wife was curious, silently looking on. Her husband closed his eyes and lifted his right hand, to mark off a circle. His lips moved in correspondence with the hand, counting, counting.

Then suddenly his eyes opened and he shouted, "I've got it. I've got it!"

"Got what?" his wife asked.

"Just exactly what we want!" In a dash he was into his car, waving a goodbye kiss. The roar of the blue Oldsmobile engulfed the adagio admonition from Mrs. Rossi, "Drive carefully!"

As soon as Anthony Rossi reached his large office, a corner room in the staff building at Tropicana, he phoned for one of his expert engineers. Taking his pen and a sheet of paper, he drew a sketch of a circular decorator machine planned to silk-screen the glass bottles at 300 per minute.

"But Mr. Rossi," his engineer warned, "it isn't possible."

"Possible? Of course it's possible. Look, here's the way it will go!"

Somehow the incredulous engineer felt compelled to try. "Maybe the boss has come up with another first!" he told himself, taking the stance of his leader in this debate. He did try. The two of them worked together. And the day came when a new decorator machine fitted into its place in the march of the glass bottles from their origin in a drop of flame to completion as filled chilled juice, capped and ready for marketing.

The new machine worked like a clock. A bottle entered the circle to scoot along the miniature merry-go-round. At the right instant it was brushed with the swish of green ink labeling it with Tropicana's logo, a little girl with a basket of oranges on her head. Each bottle then trotted out of the circle into line to swing along the conveyor to the juicer, to the cap, and on to follow its particular packaging destination.

Years later, Anthony was host to a dinner guest in his home. Somehow the conversation underscored the subject of answers to prayer. "If any man lack wisdom, let him ask of God," someone quoted.

"Right," Anthony reminisced, recalling that it was patented in the name of Anthony T. Rossi for Tropicana Products, Inc.

"I've got it! I've got it!" he said. He was exuberant. Everyone present realized Anthony's wonder at God's answer to a challenge. As this incident came to mind, it was in the context of what God had done. He was not crediting himself.

The surprise and joy of that morning is indelible—another time when faith in a real and living God had proved him so.

Dinner at the White House

THEY HAD JUST STEPPED into the scintillating glory of the White House Lincoln Room in the north portico. Could it be they, themselves, Anthony and Sanna, present at this fairyland scene? Shimmering light from ceiling and walls, the splendid array of ten large round tables aglow with candles and the elegant, ornate White House plates and crystal goblets. A long table stretched the length of the back wall of the dining hall and faced the round tables.

Even now, the President and Mrs. Nixon with their honored guests were seated. On the President's right sat Sir Edward Heath, Prime Minister of Great Britain. Next to him was the Countess of Cromer, her beauty enhanced by the Rothschild jewels she wore. At the President's table were also Sir Alec Douglas Hume, the Home Secretary for Foreign and Commonwealth Affairs, and Sir Burke Trend, Secretary to the Cabinet, and many others.

Guests at the circling round tables had been invited to dine with the President as he honored England's chief of state.

Anthony, directed by the card in its minute envelop handed him, sat at table two. A Mr. Roy Ashe jovially introduced himself and engaged Tropicana's president in conversation.

Sanna's small card placed her at table six, a table close to the long host table facing them. Still disbelieving the event to be real, she glanced at the floor to see if her cream-colored deliso pumps were glass instead. Another Cinderella dream?

The trumpeters at the door startled the low murmur of one hundred and ten guests into abrupt silence. They watched as lithe violinists in tuxedos marched into the room playing, one at each of the ten round tables. The violins were exquisite. The melody—what was it—Mozart? So silver, liquid, clear, pouring forth the joy of this moment.

Like magic, every face among the scores of guests was a reflection of unclouded joy—lifting, irresistible, buoyant gladness. For wasn't this that dinner (quoting the next "Evening Star and Daily News") that even the four hundred could not make?!

How had this happened, and especially to the Anthony Rossis whose names appeared in the White House guest list the next day, February 2, 1973?

At 1800 Point Pleasant Avenue in Bradenton Florida, winter that day in late January 1973 was like a day in June. Florida was a pleasure to all its visitors for the season. At noon, Anthony drove into the garage and came into his home by the back door as usual. It was lunchtime. Mary, the maid of almost thirty years, had a green salad ready for him to toss. He walked the long narrow hall, passed by the kitchen and dining area, walked through the large living room to the front hall closet. Putting on his gray cashmere vest, he looked up, greeting his wife, "Any special mail today?"

"Why yes, Nino, look!" She handed him a large letter stamped in golden print at the upper left, "The White House." With trembling hands, they opened the frosty, crepe-textured envelope. There it was. To read and read again! Still unbelieving, Anthony spoke, "Invited to have dinner with the President in the White House"?

Sanna mentioned details as she read, " 'February 1, Thursday evening, Black tie.' It's a dinner honoring the prime minister of England, Sir Edward Heath!"

Anthony thought a few silent minutes. Like Sanna, he was beginning to wonder about preparations, proper dress and travel plans. Then he said with finality, "You know, if we are invited by the President and Mrs. Nixon, we cannot refuse."

Another small note slipped from the envelope, "Please send response to the Social Secretary at the White House at your earliest convenience."

From this point, the White House evening absorbed thought and energy for the Rossis. So few days between January 24 and February 1. Anthony's tuxedo and accessories were promptly acquired. And Tina, Anthony's stylish and attractive niece, came to Aunt Sanna's rescue. Right away they set out to find a proper dress. Tina knew the fashionable shops in St. Petersburg, and they spent most of the day there, but had to return to Bradenton empty handed.

Aunt Sanna was not the tall, slender model like Tina. Furthermore, at age fifty-five she was a 16 or even 16 1/2 for most dresses.

But they could not give up, and so sped on to Sarasota's St. Armand's Circle in the late afternoon for one last look. There, at last, they found the dress, the prettiest of all, a perfect fit. A small shop called "The First Lady" catered to half sizes. The gown selected had a fitted bodice covered in amber and orchid sequins, as was also its mandarin collar. The long sleeves were also sequined halfway to the elbow. The lined frock had a full, soft flowing crepe de chine cream skirt to the ankles.

Tina suggested that Aunt Sanna take along another dress as well. It was also a rich ivory in color, but very simple, tailored, lined and with a jacket of the same material. "I hope Uncle Nino likes the sequined dress," Tina commented, "but he may prefer the plainer style." To the glee of both Tina and Aunt Sanna, Anthony chose the beautiful, sequined one as his first choice.

Only a little while later, the Rossis were in Washington's cold drizzle. But nobody cared about the weather. They could sense the very heartbeat of America here.

At the Madison Hotel on 15th and N Streets N.W., tokens of welcome awaited the Rossis when they reached their room. A card with diagonally handwritten words in blue spelled out, "Delighted you are here!"

A few hours of pounding heartbeat hence, Anthony and Sanna were received at the White House east entrance. They met a reception with protocol worthy of a President's hospitality. Beautiful young men and women reached out to take coats, and to usher unencumbered guests into the golden East Room of the President's home.

The Rossis took one step over the threshold of that East Room doorway and were startled to hear, at megaphone volume, "Mr. and Mrs. Anthony Rossi." A roomful of strangers soon became happily conversant by the charm and thoughtfulness of the young people appointed to see that introductions were adequate and that no couples were left awkwardly alone.

The room filled quickly—senators, congressmen, secretaries of state for both Britain and the United States. The Rossis found themselves talking vivaciously with the mayor of Houston, Mr. William Farish, when suddenly all audible words fell mute. An awesome sensation swept over the hushed guests. All eyes were fixed upon the entrance when flag bearers marched in with the stirring herald band playing "Hail to the Chief." Following came the President, First Lady, Sir Edward Heath, the Countess of Cromer and others. They formed a reception line to welcome each guest.

All were carefully instructed that the gentleman must precede his wife in line as this is protocol in the United States. Handshakes were cordial if words were few. Smiles on all faces had "God Bless America" in their eyes. Anthony was close to tears, Sanna too. The surge of patriotism was overwhelming. When the Rossis got to President Nixon, and their names were cued, Mr. Nixon looked at Anthony, took his hand and graciously added the words, "From Florida." The Rossis felt themselves to be friends and not strangers here.

"Yes, this is real," the Rossis convinced themselves as the violins stopped playing. They were indeed in the dining hall of the President.

Deft waiters removed the ornate plates and set before

each guest his first course: "Supreme Pompano Meuniere." Of course, it was superb. But to Anthony it was plain to see just how the fish had been prepared. From this time forth at 1800 Point Pleasant, the Rossi's table would add a new dish, "Fish White House."

The dinner was perfect. And the menu written in artistic French included its original chef and the date on which it was created. Dessert was most innovative of all the delightful items. It was Glâce Nougatine with Petit Fours. The caramelized basket held folds of French vanilla ice cream ribboned in caramel and topped with whipped cream. Each person helped himself from the basket as the waiter gracefully proffered it.

More exciting even than the food were the toasts to the Queen and the President among other speeches from the President's table.

Too soon all was over in the Lincoln Room. Anthony and Sanna, holding their demitasse of expresso, walked the wide portrait-hung corridor to the East Room once more in the midst of all this evening's guests.

Everyone sat on a tier of seats facing the grand piano and platform from which the United States Army Chorus sang zestful songs including Mr. Nixon's favorite, "Stout-hearted Men." In honor of England's Prime Minister they closed with "Hail Britannia."

Like a fantasy, the glorious hour slipped back toward yesterdays. At about 11 P.M., the Rossis were in the ordinary taxi spinning along the slick, light-streaked route to the Madison.

Yet the reality so cherished could never vanish—a memory so valued, so significant would always remain. That tangible feel of the nations pulse, the lights in the night, could never distance themselves from two, at least, of those one hundred ten. The President had introduced his guests as "The one hundred and ten most important people in America tonight."

Right Man
Wrong Church

SUNDAY MORNING OPENED with special anticipation. The Rossi's schedule was to be quite different. Anthony had arranged for a substitute to teach his Sunday-school class at Calvary Baptist Church. He had promised to speak at one of the Black churches in town.

"Anthony, are you sure of how to get to the church where you will preach today?"

"Of course," he said. "I know the church. Right next to Mary's church, you remember. It's the one we helped with a building program several months ago."

"Oh," his wife added, "that church is called Gethsemane." And finding the address in the phone book, she noted, "It's on the corner of 5th Street and 9th Avenue West."

"Johnny is coming by to go with us, you know," Anthony spoke with a touch of excitement. His wife accepted the fact that they were in control of things. A thought had passed like a leaf in the breeze. "Maybe I should have double checked." But her husband was in a hurry.

"Are you ready? It's time to go!"

"Yes, And you have your Bible, your notes?"

"Everything." He was confident.

But little did they realize then that the church which had issued the invitation to speak at a young people's rally was not Gethsemane on 5th Avenue. St. Paul's Missionary Baptist at 525 9th Avenue East was rapidly filling up. The pastor, satisfied that he did not have to preach today, was more freehearted and jovial than usual. They were ready for opening hymns when the Rossis arrived—alas, not at St. Paul's, but at Gethsemane.

Johnny, Sanna and Anthony slipped into the church and sat on the front pew near the entrance on their left. Mary was there also. Mary Daughtry, their loyal maid and friend, had sneaked away from Ward Temple next door to join the congregation at Gethsemane.

After a bit, the guest speaker and his companions began to feel uneasy. No one stepped forward to welcome them. No one approached the speaker to brief him as to the procedure this morning.

Instead, a group of people, men and women attired in long terrycloth robes, began to huddle together watching two men calmly lift the wide plank flooring of the bare platform. Underneath was the baptistry. Evidently a baptismal ceremony would begin their services today.

It was Mary who first sensed something going wrong. She

got up and went to find the pastor. In no time, she was back to tell Mr. Rossi, "They do not expect a guest speaker here today."

Mortified, the Rossi party made their departure through the left front door, fervently hoping they escaped inconspicuously.

Outdoors and at a distance from Gethsemane, they whispered. "What church do you suppose it is?" They looked at Mary, dressed so attractively in her navy blue, not her usual white uniform, wearing a matching broad-brimmed hat.

"Mary, it wasn't Ward Temple, was it?"

"Oh, no ma'am," she was sure.

"Mary," Mr. Rossi spoke this time, keeping his voice calm and matter-of-fact. "Is there another church near here?" And he stopped. What more could he say?

"Maybe St. Mary's is it."

"Yes, St. Mary's," Mr. Rossi grabbed the idea. "That's it probably. Now tell us where it is!"

"St. Mary's is on 1st Street. I believe it's at 10th Avenue. You'll find it!"

By now the Rossi party was late although they had reached Gethsemane ahead of time. Also, by this hour, St. Paul's were fifteen minutes into their preliminaries, and no guest speaker had appeared.

Anthony, Johnny and Sanna fluttered away to their car and drove as quickly as possible to find St. Mary's. Parking was no problem. Yet the service had already begun.

"You both sit in the back," Anthony suggested, "and I will go into the side door at the front."

By the time his wife and Johnny were seated (Mary had not followed them from Gethsemane), Mr. Rossi rushed through the door near the podium, ran up onto the platform and, as the pastor turned to see him, the guest speaker apologized in a stage whisper, "I'm so sorry I am late!"

"Late? For what?" Too stunned to reply the guest found himself propelled into a private room behind the pulpit and out of view as an astonished congregation gasped at this unexpected episode. Mr. Rossi of Tropicana was always recognized by everyone in Bradenton. His picture frequently appeared in newspapers when the company won new recognition for its innovative progress.

In the back room, the preacher of St. Mary's said, "Maybe you should telephone St. Paul's." They did. Ringing on and on, their phone drew no response. Nobody was near it. By this time, St. Pauls was in the throes of perplexity, and ushers stood outside to watch Ninth Avenue traffic. They strained to spot a blue Oldsmobile coming from the west.

"Well," parlayed St. Mary's pastor, "will you preach for us today? We will be pleased if you will."

Anthony serenely obliged. "Look, this must be where the Lord wanted me to speak. See, my check is made out to St. Mary's."

"Right," the preacher laughed. "You are our pastor today." The two men emerged, jovially, from the back room, and St. Mary's pastor eloquently introduced the speaker of the day as the Reverend Anthony T. Rossi. His wife and his friend, John Douglas, were then ushered down the long red-carpeted aisle to the side front pew of the church.

Once into his message, the guest speaker had much to say. His audience was intent on every word. At last, this Sunday morning began to shine gladness again.

Later, at home and after lunch, Anthony found a letter on his desk. "Oh my! The pastor at St. Paul's was expecting me today!" Anthony went straight to the phone and called the pastor's home.

"Hello, this is Mr. Rossi."

"Oh, Mr. Rossi, I could take your head off! We had a full house. Mostly young people. And besides, I was not prepared to preach today!"

"I am so sorry," came the barely audible and penitent reply. "Will you forgive me? Is there any way I can redeem myself?"

"Only this," and St. Paul's preacher was jolly now. "If you will come to speak at our church next Sunday!"

"I will be glad to come." The response was cordial.

"And," the pastor warned, "it will cost you another $200. Don't forget."

"And St. Paul's may get a better sermon too," Anthony decided. "I will study even more this week."

Awards

I T WAS UNREAL. The grand horseshoe of tables dramatical-
ly decorated and flying the flags of the fifty states had seated
fifty-four of America's giants of accomplishment. Out beyond the celebrity tables were scored of round tables seating guests in the great ballroom. The banquet of the American Academy of Achievement was on in the Salt Palace.

All the way from Bradenton, Florida, to Salt Lake City,
Utah, Anthony T. Rossi was one among those to receive the
award of the Golden Plate at this annual salute to excel-
lence. Rossi sat beside Rosalind Russell, the recent recipient
of the Floyd Odium Award for her outstanding service in the
Arthritis Foundation. Around their necks, on a long red and

white and blue ribbon, hung the medal replica of the Golden Plate.

Anthony, in the dazzling lights and enchantment of the occasion, found it a moment hard to believe when Lowell Thomas presented him with the award following a glowing introduction summarizing his accomplishments in Tropicana Products, Incorporated.

No one could see, however, that Rossi had a zipper from ankle to knee to accommodate the thick white cast he wore. Only two weeks ago, he and his good friend, Ed Price, had purchased their tickets to fly to Utah for tonight's event. But meanwhile, one Saturday afternoon, Anthony had broken his ankle while working with one of his foreman on a piece of machinery at the plant.

A disturbed Ed Price phoned Rossi soon after hearing of the accident. "Tony, do you really think we can make it to Salt Lake City by July 1st?"

"Sure, Ed, no problem. And I'll promise to be using only one crutch by then."

Anthony's characteristic optimism won out. The unforgettable evening had come to pass, a gracious highlight of 1972.

This event, however, was only one of the long list of awards Tropicana's chief would receive. One of the earliest had been to be proclaimed "Man of the Year" in his own city in 1958. Later, along with others of Bradenton's benefactors, his footprint (size 13) was impressed upon the concrete sidewalk in front of the Court House facing downtown Manatee Avenue.

In 1975, Rossi received the Freedom Foundation Award.

In 1976, Anthony T. Rossi became one of the few living members to be inducted into Florida's Citrus Hall of Fame.

This honor acknowledged him as leader in Florida's citrus industry with his introduction of the first production of fresh-chilled orange and grapefruit juice. This was now the fastest growing segment of Florida's citrus industry. Honors and awards to "Mr. Tropicana" flowed neck in neck with the company's phenomenal growth.

Even after Tropicana's zenith, when *Forbes* and *Fortune* magazines, among dozens of others, retold the story, Rossi was yet to receive another unexpected honor.

It was April 26, 1980. Commencement was underway at the University of Tampa. Guests had already dined in the famous Dome Room of the college, and now, at four o'clock, they were seated outdoors in Plant Park. The dappled sun and shade of late afternoon fell gently on the large assembly facing the veranda where ceremonies would be held. Sanna Rossi with Mary Ellen Germany, Faith and Ken Barnebey, sat in one of the back rows. Behind them on their left, a large ornate fountain gushed in splashing competition to speakers on the porch platform. Beyond the campus walls, horns and sirens dinned in the Tampa traffic. In fact, a curtain of varied sounds backdropped the central ceremonies of this afternoon.

Everyone stood as "Pomp and Circumstance" began. Dignitaries marched to their positions on the porch stage. Anthony Rossi was among those and would be presently introduced as the Commencement speaker.

With the solemn measures of the march, the graduates, two hundred and thirty-six young people, took their seats in front of the platform. Soon they would receive their diplomas in science, music or arts of diverse titles.

Next came the National Anthem, rousing all to their feet once more. After the invocation and formal greetings, President Cheshire addressed the graduates and guests. When the moment came for Anthony Rossi to stand behind the microphone, his audience quickly forgot the outside noises—the fountain, traffic, twittering birds in the shading oak trees. They listened. The speaker was talking to them from his heart and out of a lifetime stretching back to the very turn of the century. The young folks found it hard to realize—from 1900 until now! Certain topic sentences gripped their imaginations.

"Have a clear purpose or goal.

"Do not be discouraged. A discouraged person will never be successful.

"Be strong. Don't weaken.

"Use your common sense.

"Take care of those working with you and for you, if you are in a place of leadership.

"Be honest. Don't look back. Keep looking ahead. And remember, it is not how much knowledge we acquire, but the wisdom to use that knowledge that counts.

"And, above all, listen to God. Have faith in God. Let him guide you."

The speech was not long. When he sat down, the students stood to applaud. They genuinely appreciated the man and his guidelines given them on this new-beginning day in their young lives.

Following his address, Mr. John Germany and Mr. J. Thomas Tonchton, trustees of the university, presented Anthony T. Rossi with hood and scroll. And at this instant, he became Doctor of Humane Letters, honoris causa.

As he sat down once more, and observed each student come forward for his degree, Anthony felt both honored and humble. These young men and women had earned their rewards for studies done in the structured learning of the university. And he thought, "My learning is such contrast to theirs. I seldom went to school, even as a young boy; but . . ." And thoughts trailed into wordless awe at God's hand upon his mind and heart through the years.

The friends and colleagues of Anthony Rossi who saw what transpired this afternoon, wholeheartedly agreed that Tropicana's Chairman of the Board and Head of the Aurora Foundation had more than earned the doctorate he received today.

And for Rossi, honors and awards would continue, highlighting every year to come. His work would grow with new ideas burgeoning as he strode forward, listening to God, eager to be used of Him. Years could lengthen life, but no touch upon his spirit would be called "growing old." Young is the pace that seems to give and give again to serve God.

The Lord Is
My Shepherd

THAT THURSDAY IN FEBRUARY of 1976 had seemed a rather average day. Nothing unusual had happened. The Rossis entertained guests at noon for lunch. As they conversed, someone pointed out that three hippie-looking young men were sauntering across the backyard near the seawall of the Manatee River. Later, the same trio walked along the street in front of the house. Guests commented on this incident, but discussions of more substance flowed on into other channels. The trespassers were forgotten.

Little did the Rossis imagine that those three living in low rental apartments not far away had been fantasizing all that day about robbing the corner house at 1800 Point Pleasant where Mr. and Mrs. Rossi lived.

The evening of Thursday was quiet—occupied with happy things such as reading the day's mail, writing a letter—Anthony dictating it, his wife acting as secretary. A little past nine o'clock, Anthony said, "I must get that cassette player I promised your sister Emily. It is out in my car." He then went outside to find it. His wife heard the front door open again and close. He had returned with the player.

At about that moment, Sanna began to dial the phone number of Dorothy Brown. Her mother, Lou Stark, was in the hospital, and the Rossis wanted to find out how she was doing. The seven numbers completed, Dorothy's husband Bob responded to the ring. Just as Sanna began to talk to him, the front door bell chimed at the Rossis.

"I'll go!" and Anthony walked past the phone table near the bedroom door and out into the front hall.

Still talking to Bob, Sanna was startled by loud shouts at the front entrance, only a step away from the door near the phone. She peeped around that doorway and saw her husband in a struggle, wrestling with a tall youth, about eighteen years old. He was wearing a decent-looking light blue suit.

"Get inside!" the kid yelled.

"No, you get outside!" Anthony shouted. His wife did not see the gun in the boy's hand, but stepped back to the phone to alarm Bob Brown at the other end of the line.

"Quick," she commanded, "Call the police. Have them come, rush to our house. We have an intruder!"

Astonished, Bob declared he would. He hung up. A few seconds passed. Sanna stepped back out into the front hall.

There stood Anthony, alone. He had shoved the boy out. "He had a gun!" Eyes wide with incredulity, he drew a deep breath. "And," he continued, "another man was with him—just outside the front door!"

In minutes, police sirens electrified the usually serene, reputably choice neighborhood. Two police officers came into the Rossi home to talk with them. One officer left immediately with Anthony along to join the search. The other officer stayed with Mrs. Rossi.

The alert policeman immediately spotted the long knife dropped on the front yard. Also, a neighbor across the street reported seeing two men race over her yard, headed for the large apartment building across the street at the east side of her house.

This pointed the police to the very place where one of the intruders lived. Quickly the policeman was able to locate the suspect's apartment and demanded permission to search. They found nothing, but kept looking around. When they walked into the bathroom, they noticed the tub was full of laundry. Underneath those clothes, they found their man. In less than an hour the two felons were discovered and arrested.

Next morning, Anthony Rossi went to the police station on Ninth Avenue in town. They needed him to identify the gun. A number of revolvers lay on a large counter.

"Is it this one?"

"No."

"This?"

"No."

"What about this?"

"Yes. That's the gun. I could not mistake it. I kept my eyes on it every second."

"Oh," the officer drew a deep breath. "I marvel that you are still alive! The automatic was loaded and the safety latch released. Ready to shoot."

"God kept us," Anthony replied simply.

He was thinking of Psalm 23, repeated at prayers the first thing every morning and the last thing every night. "The Lord is my Shepherd."

Anthony thought then too of much unfinished work yet to do. Blueprints for the Bradenton Missionary Village were on the top of his desk at Tropicana. So much more to attempt for God's glory!

After this break-in, a new way of life began for the Rossis. It seemed practical to take a few security measures. They added the beautiful German Shepherd, Lady Jasmine to their home. She became Lady to them. Also they installed a new security system, and for Lady's protection, they put up a high wire-mesh fence around the backyard along the seawall.

A new milestone of God's hand of protection marked that particular Thursday in the second month of 1976—a fresh commentary on that favorite psalm, "The Lord is my Shepherd."

The Tropicana Train

AT THE ROSSI HOME on Point Pleasant, the five chimes of the doorbell were ringing. It was exactly 7 P.M. "I'll go," said Anthony. In his voice a tense excitement trembled. His wife knew instinctively that a great new dream was brewing: another innovation for Tropicana, now a giant industry, doubling its total profit every two and a half years.

As he reached the front door, he apologized to his wife, "You must stay out of sight, dear. Some Tropicana officers are here to work on a new project. We'll sit around the dining room table. I'll let you know when it's time to make coffee and serve some refreshments."

"Fine," she answered, remembering the coffee was already set to plug in and goodies prepared.

The four men, including Bob Powers in charge of transport, plunged into enthusiastic discussion. With papers, drawings and other statistical materials they gave themselves to intense concentration. To them this was not work, it was most stimulating mental exercise in a great innovation.

One of the company's biggest strides was in the making—the concept of the Tropicana-owned train to transport orange juice and grapefruit juice in massive volume to the New York metropolitan area and the Northeast. Since the year of the Mexico barges, Anthony had turned again to buying from the golden groves of Florida, now back to its normal production. The company put to use varied means of shipping the products—by glassed-in freight to the West, by refrigerated trucks and by piggy-back trailers on rails to the Northeast.

But only a week ago, Rossi had exploded, "Our volume is too great! We need a larger transport facility!" And he talked with Powers about returning to ship transport in bulk.

However, a new option pressed for attention. And the President of Sea Board Railroad came to see Tropicana's Chief. "Mr. Rossi," Bob Powers stepped forward that morning. And Anthony pushed back from his desk and stood up to greet the gentleman. Powers continued, "This is Mr. Philip Lee of Sea Board Railway."

Mr. Lee was welcomed and seated across from Rossi at the massive desk. They talked unhurriedly and without interruption. Lee pointed out that rail transport could be more feasible than ship and less expensive too.

Anthony's concern was for volume equal to or surpassing that of ship transport. Lee had his facts well in hand, and a deal was in the offing.

Now, tonight in January 1970, the men talked in careful detail, laying their plans out on the Rossi dining table. Moving forward as each aspect of the project could be agreed upon by common sense, yes, and very precise mathematics.

It was about midnight after refreshments and goodbyes. But as the friends left and before the front door closed, a whiff of Tropicana's cattle feed cooking blended with a soft salt breeze off the river a few yards away. That pleasant molasses smell of the tasty pulp roasting filled the air and brought the great plant four miles east so near.

When Anthony closed the door and commented on the evening's work, his face glowed with that flush a person feels when he knows a new first for the company is already in the works.

"We'll be meeting almost every night now for a while," he explained to Sanna. "So we had better have plenty of refreshments on hand."

Many conferences ensued. And the prospect developed into actuality. Tropicana engineers presented their plans to the Fruit Growers Express Company of Alexandria, Virginia. The rail cars were then built with special cushioning and protection devices. Back in the yards at Tropicana, the large rail cars were completed. Painted white, they wore the insignia of Tropicana; the logo, its little girl; and its trade slogan, "100 % Pure Orange Juice." Owned by the company, they were the biggest rail cars Sea Board could permit. A 1,500-foot rail spur was laid into the Tropicana property. Also, a new 144,000 square-foot cold storage plant was ready to store another 2.5 million cases of juice.

Two Sea Board Railroad engines pulled the sixty cars, loaded to the limit—a mile-long refrigerated Tropicana

"Look!" It was a summer evening and Anthony was home to see it! He pointed from the patio toward the river east. And there it was! The basso whistle roaring, the white cars rumbling across the railroad bridge. Its engines reached the north extremity of the span as the last car rolled onto the south end of the bridge.

"See the train? It measures the one-mile width of our river. They call it "The Great Snow White Train!"

The company had built 150 cars altogether. They could never use less than sixty cars for the trip to Kearney Depot in New Jersey. In thirty-six hours the cars just now crossing the Manatee would reach their northeast terminal—a long white ribbon advertizing the orange juice. At Kearney, a new storage plant was standing on a seventy-acre tract with 57,600 square feet under roof and 5,400 feet of private rail track. Dock space there was also sufficient to load eighty refrigerated trucks heading for deliveries to New England markets.

The White Train assured Tropicana both of improved quality control and increased operational efficiency. It immediately proved itself to be economical.

June 1, 1970 established a new mark for Tropicana. The first scheduled Unit Train ever to operate from Florida in the history of food industry made headlines in the world of industry. Even before 1970 closed, the company's net profits were up a whopping 85.2 per cent.

Today the mile link of rail cars still rumbles over Bradenton's beautiful Manatee in Florida's Gulf Coast area. It carries one million gallons of liquid sunshine in its streamlined carriages. The Unit Train dramatized the phenomenal growth Tropicana would achieve in the 1970s.

Yet, once to its zenith, what? Would Rossi be prepared to

meet the stampede of other industries to acquire his "Baby," Tropicana?

A hard choice would come inevitably. How would he face it? Would his indomitable faith in God's providence still hold?

What else of the 1980s? Would a new dream quicken his imagination and propel him forward, onward? "Don't look back," he often said. But looking ahead must be toward the new day, and his zeal quickened more than ever.

Tropicana Meets
Beatrice

LONDON. THE HOTEL Savoy lecture hall was filled with analysts and stockbrokers taking copious notes as they listened. The speaker was the portly but distinguished Mr. Rasmussen, president of Beatrice Foods, Inc. Anthony Rossi, next in line to speak, noted that Rasmussen was not halfway through the thick stack of notes he followed in appropriate detail. Beatrice is a very large conglomerate of Industries, Anthony realized, with dairy supplies in the midwest, to become by now a great corporation.

Rasmussen's face flushed with excitement as he talked. He himself had worked up to the top, starting at first with dairy deliveries. Today, as the executive of Beatrice Foods, he was another Alger Hiss success. Now and then his blue eyes looked up from notes to audience.

He was every whit Scandinavian and stolidly built. His speech presented Beatrice in terms the analysts wanted to hear.

Anthony looked at his watch. "The speaker is already five minutes over his allotted time," he fretted a bit inwardly. "I will need to shorten my talk." And how to do this distracted his thoughts from the Beatrice report at least momentarily.

Five more minutes ticked away, still talking. Anthony's concern seemed to be shared now with some in the packed hall. Others were time conscious too.

"Fifteen minutes overlap," Rossi was alarmed. "I'll need to cut my speech in half." And then, abruptly, the Beatrice president sat down under a saltshaker spread of polite applause.

Anthony T. Rossi of Tropicana Products, Inc., was briefly introduced, yet his introduction was definitive enough to allow him to jump into the midst of his subject without preliminary remarks. Instantly, he had his audience sitting up, intrigued. As he talked they began to see a unique concept dramatized.

The industry was self-sufficient in every way, vertically integrated to supply all its needs by manufacture within Tropicana itself. Not only was their method of processing fresh-chilled citrus juice singular, but also, its aseptic cold packaging under vacuum seal was a first in the food processing business.

"We make our own glass containers, our own plastic screw-on caps, our own juice cartons, plastic containers for other juice products and even our own cardboard boxes for shipping.

As Rossi spoke, some put down their pens and leaned forward to catch every word. They were incredulous when they heard of how the juice was transported to the great northeastern markets. A Unit Train! The first of its kind.

Anthony Rossi then underscored some of his principal guidelines: "We keep the quality of Tropicana the very best. We believe in maintaining maximum volume at lower prices than those of our competitors. Profit is due to volume as well as to our savings by producing our own supplies of containers and boxes. For the past ten years, Tropicana has doubled its profits every two and a half years."

The astounding résumé of Tropicana closed in fifteen minutes to keep within the time allotted. Rossi had spoken without too many words, saying exactly what he wanted to communicate, and with characteristic modesty. His audience was impressed. And what was that he mentioned about God? Giving God credit for his achievements? No doubt this man was Christian, pointing up a master key to his remarkable report.

When he sat down a rain of applause told him his listeners approved Florida's famous Tropicana Products, Incorporated.[4]

Afterwards, Mr. Rasmussen came up to Mr. Rossi. "Sir," he said, "I would like to come to see you in Florida in the near future."

Anthony was a bit evasive, though gracious. He sensed a new overture to join in marriage his "Baby," his now widely coveted industry.

How hard would Beatrice press for another prize to add to its complex of industries? So far, he had resisted others—Kellogg, Phillip Morris, Pepsi-Cola and many more. Anthony did as always, praying to God for guidance and protection.

On the jumbo jet crossing the Atlantic back to Florida, he mused about the future. One day, inevitably, Tropicana would be acquired. "But not now," he hoped.

Long before the plane landed in Miami, his mind and heart were back at his office into the rush and whir of decision making at Tropicana—so exciting, invigorating, provocative of new goals ahead.

From Tropicana
to Aurora

INSTEAD OF GROWING, we built a glass plant. Instead of growing, we put up a carton plant. Instead of growing, we put up a plastic plant and bought a train system." At his massive mahogany desk in his large new office, Anthony Rossi addressed the visitor sitting opposite him. He was Mr. Bob Lederer of the magazine, *Beverage World.* The exciting story of Tropicana would be the feature article for May 1977. Lederer had already chosen his title with the frontispiece picture of Anthony Rossi before a background of the tall pipes and framework of the Company's purification system. In sunshine lettering the caption would read, "It's not just for breakfast anymore." The unfolding, lengthy write-up was to be a full coverage of a most successful industry. Though Rossi was its centerpiece, the review included individuals of his magnificent team—hand-picked experts in their specific performance for Tropicana.

"We believe we're more advanced in this business than anyone. The year before last, we used 17 1/2 million boxes of oranges plus grapefruit. Last year we used 25 million. This year we will use 30 million boxes. This industry has to expand mightily in the coming years."

Anthony always envisioned more for the future. And now approaching age 78, he continued to maintain a strenuous schedule. He felt it necessary to know on a daily basis, everything going on in the business.

"Control. This is the key word," he often emphasized, "You cannot let go. You must tackle problems as they come up and work with your people in any question or difficulty they may bring to you."

The late 1970s for Tropicana were almost awesome as the success story hit the papers and leading magazines like *Forbes* and *Fortune*.

By 1978, after his London speech when Rossi introduced his company to the Beatrice Foods conglomerate, the Orange King was pushing ahead for new and bigger developments in Tropicana.

One morning, out in the plant, Anthony stood with his good friend, Frank Erdman, an expert engineer. Someone caught their picture as they looked up at the giant steel-buff silos of the industrial glass plant. Together they were supervising the completion of a third one.

"You know, Anthony," Erdman spoke out, "your idea about how to make use of gravity to avoid putting up another silo for the second plant is working perfectly."

"Good," Rossi responded simply.

"At first, I didn't think it would go. But it is a great idea. And you've saved the company a couple of million too."

Frank Erdman, who had earned degrees in engineering, was expert in his field. Yet he marveled at his chief, who, without such structured learning, could perceive innately and see new ways to do things. He had the imagination of an inventor, and could use information gleaned by reading productively, exploring projects within the Tropicana operation.

Late in the year of 1978, the Beatrice men came to see Anthony in his office upstairs in the beautiful new office building. They had come previously with overtures Rossi understood but resisted firmly. Today, they sat down in the brown leather chairs and fixed their attention on Tropicana's president and chairman of the Board.

"We are interested in buying Tropicana." They finally summed up their intentions.

"But it is not for sale," Anthony replied. He spoke decidedly.

Yet in his heart, he realized someday the company would be bought. If not directly, the bidders could bypass the Board of Directors and offer an attractive price to the public shareholders. As he studied the men before him, he felt some comfort in knowing they represented a wholesome food industry, not incompatible with Tropicana commitment to healthful beverage products. Now Anthony prayed again for guidance. At this time Tropicana shares were $36 a share. It suddenly came to him to ask for a high price, high enough, he hoped, to dismiss his Beatrice suitors.

They pressed him further. "At what price would you sell, Mr. Rossi?" "Fifty-two dollars a share!" he barked. "No more.

No less. Take it or leave it."

"We'll take it!" the three shouted in unison.

Too stunned to realize fully its significance, Anthony Rossi had just closed the Tropicana book in his life. Feeling a deep sense of peace and rightness, he stood to his feet and shook hands with his Beatrice guests.

For Anthony, the immediate future would become traumatic. Yet beyond a long, lonely hallway he would find another, a far greater opportunity to serve God. By investing much of his share from the sale of the company into two foundations, Anthony Rossi would discover more deeply than before that, "It is more blessed to give than to receive."

The Bradenton
Missionary Village

DREAMS DO COME TRUE, especially when God sketches
them across the mind and roots them in the heart. A wise
person has said that a Christian's most pragmatic wisdom is
to discover how God is moving, and to move with Him.

"When did you first think of it—the Village?" Many have
directed this question to its originator. And Anthony Rossi
answered, "I thought of it long before selling Tropicana to
Beatrice. Imagine people who have given twenty-five, thirty
years in missionary service. What will they do when they
must retire? Some may have no place to live when they
return from their fields of ministry. This is something God
wants me to do for his servants. I understand now that with

my Aurora Foundation, capital from my share of the sale of Tropicana, I can realize such a village here for retired missionaries. These are people that must have the best."⁵ The vision of a specialized housing estate did not remain long in the unseen plan of Anthony Rossi's heart.

First, land must be found. His initial purchase of property close to Bradenton proved to be too low for proper drainage. Then, later, he was able to buy 350 acres on Highway 64 from a Mrs. Chaires who wanted to sell off her dairy cattle land eight miles east of Bradenton.

"We want 100 acres of this property for the village," Anthony told his contractors.

Next, blueprints on his desk began the village saga. "How many houses will there be?" someone asked. "As many as twenty-five?"

"Why," Anthony replied, "more than a hundred. And every house will become two apartments."

One Saturday morning in 1980, friends gathered at the site east of Bradenton. They came to dedicate the new enterprise to God and his blessing. A spade scooped out the first bite of earth. Great yellow earth-moving equipment was there already to throw its weight into the task. They must dig out four lakes and level the soil. Slowly, skillfully, mud and sand, large fish bones and curious fossil teeth were conquered. Dove Brothers construction men set in the essential systems for water, sewage, electricity and drainage.

Cement block and brick duplexes began to rise along the roads circling the five-acre lakes. After awhile, the large community center, the storage house and the Bible Alliance building grew to completion until one day the village stood there intact, a solid fact, a divine seal pressed into a piece of Florida ground.⁶

Along with indoor decorating of each apartment, fully equipped with household supplies, came the outdoors landscaping headed by Charlie Johnson and his crew of energetic young men. Lampposts automatically turn on each evening lighting the main boulevard, Aurora, and the avenues branching out around the village.

Harry and Bertha Liu were the first residents and represented Pocket Testament League with its work in the Orient.

As the missionaries began to make the village their home. Charlie and his workers continued planting floral landscapes and trees. Carpeted in green, the center and circumference burst into bloom.[7]

By early 1986 residents numbered one hundred plus. They were happy with a lifestyle paced to their needs. No boredom here. Jim and Renee Bigley, the managers, proved to be both dedicated and capable, so also their assistants, Ed and Barbara Dowdy.

Imaginative, creative, purposeful, these add up the quorum to vote the village alive. Its beauty has the open smile of heaven upon it. Life in the Avenues A, B, C and D is neighborly, caring and sympathetic. Helping one another constrains everyone because they belong to each other as a family.

The village reveals how missionaries do not retire. Some from Spanish fields seek out local Spanish-speaking people to befriend and teach. Others discover Haitians like those they knew on the island. Some work with children's classes in town and in local Sunday schools. Several are writing articles and books of substantial value to share with many. Everyone entertains visitors frequently. And the village has already become a reservoir of spiritual leadership to a wide span of Bradenton area churches. Now within one-third of its actual capacity, the missionary housing estate represents more than twenty-five mission organizations in united diversity and dynamic.

Village recreation includes swimming (they have two pools), shuffle boarding, bicycling, strolling, gardening, crafts, hymn sings, and community center celebrations of birthdays, anniversaries, seasonal activities. It is ideal for special films, travelogs, lectures and varied festivities. Each Friday morning the prayer breakfast ties everyone together.

To some, work is recreation when it is assembling cassette albums in the Bible Alliance building. Every day, shipments are made ready to go out to the blind who order the materials and to the prison chaplains in North America who are eager to receive this help in their responsibilities.

An alert security guard watches over Bradenton Missionary Village day and night. No one unauthorized may enter and only one entrance operates. A car may come into the village only if the guard-house button is pushed to lift the barricade at the one gate.

But once on the Aurora Boulevard beyond the lifted bars, this heaven-ceiled suburb spreads out, set in green lawns and floral garden spots, citrus trees, lakes, graced with fountains and swirling sea birds. Surrounding the lakes are the houses. At night, lampposts begin to glow when the evening canopy is starlit above them. Often residents have stated, "For us, this is the very threshold of heaven."

Bible Alliance—
A New Direction

THEIR PLANE OUT OF Denver flew west at an altitude above palisades of cloud, intensely white and sculptured beneath the wide wings on steadfast course. "Can you believe we are actually going to be landing in Fresno within forty minutes?"

Anthony heard the question, his wife guessed. But he seemingly snoozed. She knew though that their brief vacation would not be purposeless. None was ever goalless. Her husband was not actually asleep. Thoughts carefully, logically built would sometime spring forth. A new surprise venture! "What," she wondered, "is brewing now along with the reassuring hum of the jet?"

As anticipated, Georgia and Joe Aleppo met their Uncle Nino and Aunt Sanna with much enthusiasm. *Molta felicita!* Nothing could quite equal the fervent welcome Italiano style! And the Rossis were soon into a glorious California holiday—only it would be contained, travel included, within the limit of five days.

The Aleppos kept interesting things happening—trips to the giant Sequoias and Yosemite, a look at Fresno's zoo, luncheon one day with Carmelo and Natalie (Georgia's brother and wife). Carmelo was already packing to return to Sicily with his children and his mother, Teresa Solarino, Anthony's youngest sister. She eagerly anticipated getting back to her home in Acereale near Catania, Sicily. There she could understand the language—her own tongue, and become reunited with old friends.

The Fresno vacation with Georgia and Joe allowed for unhurried conversations at the breakfast table. There Uncle Nino's concealed goals were uncovered. "I have been thinking very much, Joe, Georgia, about directing our Bible Alliance work to concentrate on the blind. The more I consider this, the more logical it seems to me. They are the ones who may love the most the spoken New Testament. In fact the whole Bible. Also the messages done by Dr. Di Gangi, for example, may be treasured by them."

"Why, Uncle Nino, that sounds to me a great idea!" Joe Aleppo's response was echoed by his wife. Georgia was just as excited about it as her husband was. And they listened as Uncle Nino continued.

"We can send them to those who do not have access to these words except by hearing. I believe this is the way the Lord is directing us to go."

At this point the animated conversation paused. One of

those long "Selah's" gave space for thought, for prayer. Finally, Joe spoke into the quiet, "You know, Uncle Nino, I believe you are precisely on the right track. This sounds very good to me." And Uncle Nino took a long look at his niece and her husband.

"Georgia, Joe, I know you are very busy here with the ranch and the business of harvesting grapes for raisins. But whenever you have some time, I have things for you to do for Bible Alliance."

"Uncle Nino," Joe was earnest, "soon the farm will become dormant. We will have time then. Besides, we have been exasperated with this raisin business. Competition is so sharp that we barely break even with it profit-wise."

"Well, Joe," his uncle counseled, "you have given it a try for many years now. Since it is not proving worthwhile, would you consider selling the farm? I need a couple to help Bible Alliance full-time. I am not thinking only of supplying cassettes to the blind, because I believe there is also a strategic use for them in the prisons of the United States. When you can, I need you and Georgia to explore both of these avenues. The State of California could be our first test. Just to see what happens."

Back in Florida, the Rossis found themselves wonderfully refreshed by those days in the fruit-filled valley floor below the grand Sierra Nevada ranges west of Del Ray where the Aleppos enjoyed a rambling ranch-style home.

At least twice a week, Uncle Nino talked with the Aleppos in California. Conversations concerned teaching cassette albums for prison chaplains and for the blind.

"What have you found out, Joe?" came the query from Florida.

"Oh, Uncle Nino, we were cordially received here in Fresno by the Fellowship Center for the Blind. They gave us names from the Library for the Blind and directed us to a network of centers in the state. We find they are well organized with centers covering the central valley. Also, we have other connections for Sacramento."

Uncle Nino listened in rapt silence. Only a yes here and there assured Joe and Georgia he was still on the line. When he said goodbyes, the hour in Bradenton was late. Presently, sleep couched beautiful new dreams. A new project had taken off with winged feet. The tide was of God. And Bible Alliance would mount its magnificent crests with increasing joy.

Phone calls from California became more and more exciting. "Uncle Nino," Georgia and Joe rejoiced, "the Center for the Blind in LA. has called us. 'Please come, we beg you,' they say. We are in Los Angeles now. We went to the Braille Institute on Vermont Avenue. They were 100% enthusiastic. Big crowds came for our first distribution of the albums. We need Spanish cassette albums, as well, Uncle Nino."

In Florida, at his bedside phone table, Anthony wrote down the orders his nephew stated. With a sigh of thanksgiving he told Joe and Georgia, "We'll send them right away. Also we are excited about how prison chaplains out there are becoming interested. This makes me very happy."

When he hung up the phone, Anthony glowingly said to his wife, "It is wonderful what the Lord is doing out there in California."

Months passed, ten months in fact. And the Aleppos had covered most of California. Now they were focusing attention on statewide conventions. They were discovering that ministry to the blind was organized on a nation-wide scale.

Eventually, the new work would cut them loose from the ranch in Fresno. They sold it and moved to Bradenton to head up Bible Alliance, adding more staff as the work developed. By Christmas 1985, the Aleppo family was settled in Florida.

But before this climactic sequence to their work, Joe and Georgia phoned Uncle Nino at his office. It was in July of 1984.

"Uncle Nino, we need you very much to join us at the Convention for the Blind in Springfield, Missouri. We will go ahead. They have a display table for us. If you can come this Friday, we will meet your plane. You will only need to be away for the one week. Get a return ticket for Sunday afternoon. Can you come?"

With no hesitation, feeling weariness slip from his shoulders, Uncle Nino consented. "Yes, of course I can come. I will be there Friday."

Materials had all been mailed ahead and were there for the Aleppos to explain to everyone interested in signing for them. This was the National Church Conference for the Blind. All guests could be accommodated for meals and activities at their headquarters in the Church of God.

Before Anthony left for Springfield, Joe and Georgia warned him, "You will see that is is hard to convince these people that the albums are free of charge. We need you here to help us prove this point."

Anthony thought, in contemplating the Springfield trip, "How glad I am that God allows me to see his blessing to sightless people. His word can comfort them."

And, Anthony Rossi, no matter how busy the Aurora office, had determined to join the Aleppos in Springfield, Missouri.

A Matter of Priority

ANTHONY STEPPED INTO his spacious office on Sixth Avenue West at about 9:00 A.M. Warmth and cheer greeted him. The Aurora Foundation staff came alive with smiles and "Good mornings." He glanced at the crystal and gold clock on his wide desk. Yes, 9:05 A.M. Letters neatly stacked caught his attention. Always much to do. A small computer printed out in electric green data pertinent to current investment interests. The Foundation, committed to an ever increasing budget, must carry sufficient profit to function well and avoid draining their capital.

Echoes of his Tropicana days decorated the office walls—the ship, the train and the Golden Plate Achievement award.

A gift from Bolivia missionaries hung there too—a large horsehead mat done in genuine horsehair. Taking more wall space was a large water color of a rainy day in Paris. Prominent too was the airplane view of Bradenton Missionary Village.

Wine-colored leather desk chairs and couch contrasted brightly with the royal blue carpeting. He sat down at the desk. And, *presto,* the phone rang. He picked it up. His thoughts were filled with plans for the trip tomorrow. The Bible Alliance New Testament albums would be displayed at the convention for the blind. This new absorbing interest lifted his spirit, though he had been feeling tired lately. It was a Thursday morning in July 1984.

"Hello," Anthony responded to the beige phone in his hands. He was surprised to hear the voice of his heart specialist in Lakeland.

"Mr. Rossi, we want you to come to the hospital tomorrow morning. But don't be worried. Your latest phone check of your nine-year old pacer shows it slowing down."

"Oh," Anthony sounded tentative.

"It is important that we replace it with a new one immediately. May we expect you tomorrow?"

Anthony hesitated, then replied in a soft, gently persuasive tone, "But, Dr. McIntosh, I can't come tomorrow. I will be in Springfield, Missouri, at a convention for the blind."

"You mean," Dr. Henry McIntosh paused, "you are flying to Springfield tomorrow?"

"Yes. People from all over America will be there. I am to join my nephew, Joseph Aleppo. He says it is important for me to be there."

"When will you return?" the doctor spoke firmly.

"Sunday evening." Anthony spoke without a trace of concern—upbeat as usual.

"In that case," his doctor advised, "may I expect you to enter Lakeland Hospital Monday afternoon?" He got an agreeable, matter-of-fact yes.

"I will see you then," Dr. McIntosh concluded. "We have a new pacer for you. The operation will be early Tuesday morning. Better count on being out of the office for three or four days."

As Anthony cradled the phone, he told his secretary, Sharon Weaver, to make note of his hospital date "first thing next week."

Thursday scurried by, loaded with decisions: helping ones, useful ones, fanning out across a varied spectrum of assists—little and big, in town, at the village and to the ends of the earth.

Mailings of New Testament cassette albums had already reached Springfield. In fact, Georgia and Joe were there busily presiding over the Bible Alliance table. They would meet Uncle Nino's plane soon.

So many things wrought by prayer alone would follow and precede the tall, slender confident traveler. A distinct purpose in his soul fed and nourished his unintimidated spirit. He had a winner's point of view!

But quickly enough Sunday evening brought Anthony back home, more than ever encouraged over the response of many blind people at the convention. Some could hardly be convinced that the albums were free. "These readings of the New Testament by Cliff Barrows of the Billy Graham Team, free?"

Anthony had tried to explain how the Bible Alliance Foundation was his means of providing this service. It was another fruit from the sale of Tropicana Products. Even so, after he explained this, a few still expected to find bills in their mail when they got back home.

But blind faces lighted up when they held an album in their hands—the entire New Testament to hear on their own players.

Anthony noted with comfort this quality compensation to their physical condition. He admired their spunk, their ability to smile and to be glad.

Monday he was safely in the Lakeland Hospital. Tuesday the surgery went well. After two days monitoring the new pacemaker, he was home in Bradenton—a piece of the sunshine state and a part of Florida's best to give and to be.

More Health for
the Soul

FOLLOWING HIS PACEMAKER surgery, August 19-23 came
into view soon enough. The date was a new imperative.
Around the World Travel Agency (a business belonging to
Anthony's niece, Tina Riegler) made more plane tickets for
Uncle Nino. This time Anthony was in flight to San Antonio,
Texas. Traveling was not something he particularly enjoyed.
But this trip was a must. Again the Aleppos had reached
there first and would meet the flight from Florida.

As Anthony pillowed his head and closed his eyes, he was
relaxed. "God is doing wonderful things!" he mused. Under
his seat was a small briefcase with essentials for the two or
three days he would stay in Texas. Already his thoughts

eclipsed home and office in Bradenton and drew him into interesting reverie.

"How it all started," he thought, "was really spectacular!" And he remembered those California phone calls to 1800 Point Pleasant in Bradenton. Joe and Georgia were exploring the state's prisons. Everywhere they went they found chaplains eager for the ministry offered to them by Bible Alliance.

"It has great potential," Chaplains agreed. "And we need help very much. So many prisoners are youth arrested because of drug use. We also want the Spanish albums you have," they said, stating the high percentage of Hispanics in their custody.

As Georgia and Joe visited place after place, their zeal for the work ran high. They wholeheartedly shared Uncle Nino's vision for getting a player and albums (both Bible and teaching) into the hands of prison chaplains. And at the present time, a national convention for all United States chaplains was on at San Antonio. The request was irresistible coming from his nephew, "We need you to be here, Uncle Nino. We need you very much."

The flight had seemed short, and at the San Antonio airport, Joe and Georgia rushed to greet Uncle Nino and quickly escort him to the La Quinta Hotel.

"At the convention center tomorrow, you will meet many chaplains, Uncle Nino. Those we have talked with so far are keen to meet you. As you see, Georgia and I, we are excited about this!"

The morrow came, a new gift from heaven into time on earth. And it was a perfect day. The sun was bright; the weather, not too warm for August.

Anthony and the Aleppos found their Bible Alliance spot

in the large convention hall. But they did not have long to wait alone with their display of materials. Chaplains circled them, delighted to hear what this Mr. Rossi from Florida had to tell them. Soon sheets of paper filled with orders to be shipped from Bradenton to each chaplain scattered over the fifty states.

"I'm glad I came, Joe, Georgia!" their uncle whispered. "This is greater than I had ever imagined."

"Yes, and Uncle Nino, did you hear the announcement last night that the next national convention, the winter convention, is to be in Orlando, Florida, in January 1985?"

From this point, the orders and responses intensified from America's prison chaplains. New office space in Bradenton had to be added.

With the winter convention in Florida a new thing happened. Georgia and Joe attended it, though Uncle Nino, down with flu, was told by his doctor, Willis Harris, he must treat fever with antibiotics and bed rest. No travel. Nevertheless, when the Aleppos returned from Orlando, Anthony realized another red letter day had dawned. Joe said, "You know, Uncle Nino, not only Protestant chaplains were interested this time, but nearly all the Roman Catholic chaplains as well. These signed up to receive the sound player and the Old and New Testament cassettes."

By 1986, new office space was built on to the 1115 6th Avenue West Aurora Foundation and Bible Alliance headquarters. An attractive couple, Dan and Diane Madison also moved from Fresno to join Bible Alliance staff, now directed by Joseph Aleppo.

From the downtown office, orders are relayed to the large Bible Alliance facility at Bradenton Missionary Village. There, volunteer assembly work has increased from one day weekly to three with at least twenty workers. The place hums with purposeful activity, carried forward largely by missionaries from the village itself. They keep abreast of orders. And out they go, daily, to the chaplains and to the blind requesting them.

Recently, at a birthday celebration at the village recreation hall, Anthony spoke to them, one hundred and twenty or more by this time, September 1986. He defined his contemporary enterprises like this: "In Tropicana, I had the pleasure of providing orange juice, a product healthful for the physical life. But today, mine is the greater pleasure to be providing that which can bring health to the soul."

Amsterdam '86

As 1986 HAD BEGUN, a new challenge came to Bible Alliance, a new deadline to meet. In July, the International Conference of Itinerant Evangelists, Amsterdam '86, would take place. Thousands of itinerant evangelists from the Third World would be attending. And the Graham team wanted the albums, "All you can send, and in all languages you have."[8] They would number at least 10,000. "Also," Cliff Barrows relayed the plea, "we must have at least 6,000 sound players."

"We can't send that many players!" Anthony told Barrows at first. But later, realizing the urgency and splendid opportunity involved, he consented. "You shall have 6,000 cassette players," he promised. "They can be used with 110 or 220 volt electricity, or with batteries, or without either electricity or battery since they will operate just as well by hand. I feel we must rally behind this effort and supply the evangelists with these tools."

This signaled the work force at the village. They must check each player thoroughly to assure its perfect performance overseas. Also, thousands of albums must be filled according to the exact order from the Graham Team.

Out at Bible Alliance plant in the Village, volunteers rushed forward to meet this urgency. And, at the right date in May, huge containers were packed for shipping and taken in giant trailers to the port at Savannah, Georgia. Bible Alliance met the deadline.

In July, thousands from Third World lands rejoiced when each one opened his bag of helps. Pulling out of it the sound player and bright blue albums of the spoken Bible, they laughed with gladness. "These are the greatest!" they exclaimed, one after another. "The best of all! How it will draw our people to hear the Word!"

News articles and reports of Amsterdam '86 told the same story. Six thousand evangelists were ecstatic with these gifts for their ministries. Many pictures tell the joy as well. Some close-up photos sent by John Kyle of InterVarsity Christian Fellowship eloquently reveal the impact of these special gifts worldwide.

Bible Alliance was rewarded to see its contribution toward global evangelism. Anthony read reports from the convention and smiled—"I'm glad," he answered. "God has allowed us to tangibly impact his ongoing Good News reaching the world. And this is what Aurora Foundation and Bible Alliance are all about."

On Anthony Rossi's desk at the Aurora office is, invariably, a stack of letters. "One foot high!" he declared. "Unbelievable!" Joe Aleppo had just come in with another sheaf of thank you letters. Some included additional orders. His uncle took the letters as Joe handed them to him. "These letters often make me cry," Uncle Nino commented.

"Yes," Joe answered. "They affect me the same way."

"And just look at this! We have more than three hundred requests for the cassette albums just coming in today's mail."

As Joe left to go back to his own office, Anthony picked up one of the letters off the pile. The writing was in large script and the lines were not perfectly straight. He read, "Adequate words cannot be found to express my joy and delight for the precious gift given me. It thrills my heart exceedingly to hear the Word of God read and taught. I listen prayerfully and intently."

At this moment the telephone rang. Anthony was briefly interrupted.

"Yes," he responded. "You may come to see me at two o'clock." A friend wanted to present a local worthwhile community project and need for funds.

Back to the letters, he glanced through them. All repeated the words, "Thank you."

Anthony talked silently to God that same feeling of gratitude. "I thank thee for allowing me the privilege to send lasting light to those who are blind."

By now the crystal clock pointed to 5 P.M. Anthony tidied his desk, and left his office for home. The day had passed swiftly. Yet its measured gift of time had been worthily used.

This was Friday, September 12. "Tomorrow is Saturday. But I will have work to do at the village." Preparations were underway for dining service—one hot meal a day for the missionary residents. It was to open for buffet lunch by Tuesday, September 30.

Looking ahead, planning new ventures, kept Anthony moving forward with youth in his soul and fresh ambition invigorating his mind.

At home he was glad for a brief rest before a light supper. The evening was always pleasant, with family visiting, phone calls or letter writing. Sometimes a football game or a National Geographic documentary would be interesting.

However, he was, as usual, eager for the next day to begin. "I have much to do!"

Another Day Begins

SATURDAY MORNING breakfast was always a little later, the schedule more relaxed. It was September 13, 1986: Anthony's birthday. He was actually 86 today, after saying so throughout the year. Now, he entered another year to begin with zest. Sometimes reminiscing was fun, but looking ahead was still better, more characteristic of him.

He placed his coffee cup back in its saucer. Breakfast was over. Now it was time for devotions. His wife read from Spurgeon's *Morning and Evening.* Anthony read next, three psalms. They had just finished Proverbs and turned back to read through the Psalms again.

The final Scripture portion was a chapter in the book of

Job. His wife read the first speech of Elihu, Job 32. Their daily chapter reading was by now a long way from Genesis chapter one where they had begun.

Best of all, after Scripture readings, came that closing prayer led by the head of the home. Morning passed through the south windows from the rose garden, and light, like magic, glanced across Anthony's neat white hair. "We pray that we may do thy will and follow thy commandments . . ."

Dynamic goals give upward thrust to Anthony Rossi's daily life, keeping him vigorous and young. Each new day glows with strong purpose and the particular gift of singleness of mind. Is not this a key to achievement in every hour a day may lend?

". . . And make this day a glorious day. Amen."

Notes

[1] *Tropic Ana*—The trademark of Tropicana Products, Inc.

[2] *Dr. Stephen Olford*—Prominent itinerant preacher who brought messages at the Amsterdam '86 Conference.

[3] *Dr. Mariano Di Gangi*—Well-known preacher and seminary professor. Former pastor of Tenth Presbyterian Church of Philadelphia.

[4] *Tropicana Products, Inc.*—The fresh orange-juice firm Anthony T. Rossi began in Bradenton, Florida, that eventually was listed first among the second 500 industries showing greatest progress in the USA.

[5] *Aurora Foundation*—The foundation formed by Anthony T. Rossi that contributes to missions, Christian colleges and other charities worldwide.

[6] *Bible Alliance*—A ministry, located in Bradenton, Florida, providing cassette tapes of the Bible and Christian messages in many different languages mainly for the blind and people in prisons.

[7] *Bradenton Missionary Village*—Founded by Anthony T. Rossi to to provide retirement housing for retired missionaries.

[8] *Amsterdam '86*—The International Conference for Itinerant Evangelists sponsored by the Billy Graham Evangelistic Association held July 11-21, 1986 where 8,000 evangelists gathered in Amsterdam, The Netherlands.